Nothing Scares Me.

"Avoiding danger is no safer in the long run than outright exposure. The fearful are caught as often as the bold."

— Helen Keller

More Bestselling Titles From Scott Allan

Empower Your Thoughts

Empower Your Deep Focus

Rejection Reset

Rejection Free

Relaunch Your Life

Drive Your Destiny

The Discipline of Masters

Do the Hard Things First

Undefeated

No Punches Pulled

Fail Big

Bite the Bullet

Supercharge Your Best Life

Built for Stealth

Visit author.to/ScottAllanBooks to follow Scott Allan and stay up to date on future book releases

Nothing **Scares** Me

CHARGE FORWARD WITH CONFIDENCE,
CONQUER RESISTANCE, AND BREAK
THROUGH YOUR LIMITATIONS

by Scott Allan

ISBN eBook. 978-1-989599-16-7

ISBN Paperback. 978-1-989599-15-0

ISBN Hardcover. 978-1-989599-28-0

JOIN THE COMMUNITY OF 30,000 LIFETIME LEARNERS!

Sign up today for my **free weekly newsletter** and receive instant access to **the <u>onboarding subscriber pack</u>** that includes:

> *The Fearless Confidence Action Guide: 9 Action Plans for Building Limitless Confidence and Achieving Sustainable Results!*
>
> *The bestseller poster pack: A poster set of Scott Allan's bestselling books*
>
> *The Zero Procrastination Blueprint: A Step-by-Step Blueprint to Turn Procrastination into Rapid Action Implementation!*

Begin Your Journey and Make This Life Your Own.
Click Here to <u>Subscribe Today</u> or scan the QR code below.

Contents

"Fear is good. Like self-doubt, fear is an indicator. Fear tells us what we have to do. Remember our rule of thumb: the more scared we are of a work or calling, the more sure we can be that we have to do it."

— **Steven Pressfield,** *Author of* The War of Art

Hi there, I'm **Scott Allan**, the author of *Nothing Scares Me*, and before we dive into this content, I need five minutes of your time to explain a few things about the book, and how it's emerged as one of my greatest works in the past five years.

The journey to conquer fear and all its psychological complexities has always fascinated me, for the most part because, there is a direct correlation between being scared and taking intentional action anyway. I noticed this back in 1997 when, the fear of doing anything always led to massive procrastination, followed by a tsunami of excuses that justified all the reasons why I couldn't do something.

I had a lot of ambition, but your dreams can be clouded by the fear of failure and the unknown when you let the fear in and keep courage locked out.

So, this began as a competition. Instead of giving into the fear and taking the lesser path, I would ask myself in the moment of fear: "What if I just take one small step? What if I take one tiny action towards the one thing I fear doing? What could happen?"

As my favorite author on this subject, the late Susan Jeffers has said, "We must feel the fear…and do it anyway!"

So, based on this advice, I started doing that. I began to do things that scared me anyway. What changed as a result?

As It turns out, **everything**.

A lot of people claim to have the secret sauce to defeating fear and doing miraculous things but, as a recovering fear addict who needs to keep things simple, the best strategy I learned to employ was just "Do it Anyway!"

As it happens (and I discuss in the book you're about to read), taking action builds momentum. It aligns the universe with your dreams, ambitions, and goals. You begin to realize that the fear will never go away, but is always there when we are challenged to try something new.

If your never scared in life, it could be because you're not doing anything to move to that next level.

My challenge to you is, always be scared. If it's true that people with big goals are the most frightened, set a goal so impossible to achieve that it will astonish you when you reach your destination.

I did this years ago, and twenty years later I had traveled the world, written 20+ books, and living my dreams—only because every morning I would wake up with that one big question: "What can I do today that scares me?"

Visualize the outcome as you take direct action and, regardless if you hit your target or not, it's better than standing still and doing nothing.

A Shift from the Previous Title

This book was previously titles **Do It Scared**, but with the popularity of this title appearing in other books over the years, we decided to shift away and give this book a new beginning with *Nothing Scares Me*.

The content is still the same as when it was originally published in 2017, but with a better cover and stronger appeal for a new audience that is set to crush fear and build big dreams.

Let's move forward. When you wake up, start each morning with the one simple phrase: Nothing Scares Me!

In memory of the fearless leader Susan Jeffers, let's face the fear together…and do it anyways!

Scott Allan

The Forces Holding You Back

"I have learned over the years that when one's mind is made up, this diminishes fear; knowing what must be done does away with fear."

— Rosa Parks

Imagine for a moment there is something you want so badly that it hurts to go without it. Maybe you've tried to grab that dream as it dangles in front of you, but it keeps escaping your grasp.

When people say *take direct action and just do it*, you find yourself too paralyzed to do anything. Instead, you find yourself reaching for a remote control, or killing time by immersing yourself in things that just entertain you.

As a result, you've settled for a life of good enough, and opted to live in fear

The *fear of not doing what you want to do, fear of living without,* and *the fear of growing old and never taking a chance on your future.*

Now, imagine that an invisible force is holding you back from having this one thing. It is so powerful that, no matter how hard you try to break free, it won't let you go.

That force is **fear**.

It is powerful, and for most people it is the single largest cause of self-defeat.

But, unlike most obstacles that are easy to identify, what keeps you scared is more difficult to see. We are blinded by the forces in our lives that trap us because we assume life is supposed to be this way.

When something is risky, we make excuses for why we shouldn't do it. Then, when a good opportunity presents itself, we say, *maybe next time.* But when next time arrives, there is always another excuse.

Many of us have trained ourselves to avoid the scary stuff in life, and instead, we settle for what is easy and less risky. The fear of scarcity has taken over the beauty of abundance. The result is, you create a life where you are clinging to the things that don't matter when you should be letting go.

Why Do We Trap Ourselves?

We hold ourselves back for many reasons: fear of failure, not being able to measure up, or trying to avoid looking stupid. So instead of **doing something about it**, we do nothing at all and life passes us by. Then one day you turn 50 years old. You realize you don't have much time left and you're stuck in a job, a relationship, or a situation that would have been different if you had confronted and acted on the fears that were shaping your life.

Well…

I have good news and bad news. The good news is, it's never too late to start doing the work you've always wanted to do. The bad news is, those moments you missed can never be reclaimed. But don't worry about that now. We have this day and the rest of our lives, however long that may be, to make a difference, change our behavior, take intentional action, and do the things we've always dreamed of.

From now on, you have two choices: you can either take intentional action, or do nothing at all. One path can bring you everything you've ever wanted. The other will continue to bring you more of what you've always had.

You are being held back by something that is not beyond your control. It is the result of years of conditioning and old beliefs that feed into negative thoughts about who you really are. You've been lying to yourself about how great you can be.

This doesn't have to be you anymore. We all have choices we can make in any given moment. When you think you have no choice, you are making a choice to believe that and in doing so, you're limiting your opportunities to taking the scraps left over by everyone else that got there first.

Do you want to spend the rest of your days wondering: *"What if I had…?"*

This brings us to the all-important question: Is it really life we are afraid of? Or are we just afraid to be ourselves in this life?

By the time you finish this book, you'll be doing the things you once only dreamed of. If there is any one tragedy, it is watching people live their lives in mediocrity when they have the desire to shine.

But, nobody talks about the shining greatness they could achieve. We bury what we feel passionate about because we have been told dreams are for kids. We have been told to grow up and face reality.

When we reach adulthood, it is time to get real, get an education, and get a job. I've done all these things, and even though I have no big regrets, I know that if I had stayed scared and not pursued my journey, one day I would have the biggest regret of all: I would reach the end of my life and realize that I did very little to change it.

You can change it. It is never too late to start. Life is short. Let's not waste it by staying small. There is no great fulfillment in living just half a life.

The Secret to Taking Action When Scared

When you hear about others doing things you want to do, does a pang of jealousy run through you? Don't you just want to call them up and say, "So what is your secret anyway? How is it that you did this and I didn't? What makes you better than me? What do you have that I don't?"

We often overestimate other people's abilities because it helps us deal with our feelings of failure and underachievement. When we label ourselves as failures, feelings of shame creep in. But you are not a failure. The fight isn't over until you say it is. You haven't lost anything until you decide it is time to give up. I'm betting you aren't ready to do that yet.

That is why you're here. To figure out what it is you want and how to get it. And to get it, you have to do something about your situation, life, and lifestyle. It is common for people to reach a stage in life when they look around and say, "Wait. I don't want any of this? What am I doing this for?"

Trust me. You are not alone. If you are questioning the life you have been handed, this is a good thing. It is the first step to changing it. Many people don't take that first step. They don't stop long enough to question why.

Consider this question:

How much confidence would you need to do the one thing you've always wanted to do?

In other words, *how much courage would you need to live your dream and do the things that scare you and are keeping you trapped?*

The truth is that you don't need bravery or courage. This is the illusion of confidence. For years, I believed that before I could do anything I had to be completely skilled at it so I could perform without failing. There are a lot of things we should prepare for, but perfection and being good enough before we start holds us back from doing it in the first place.

This belief that before we try it, we have to be totally perfect, full of confidence, and bursting with courage is one of the biggest lies that keeps us from doing anything, scared or not. When we are not feeling any of these things, and when we lack confidence to take action, what do we do? Something else. But the secret is so obvious that I'm sure you know it already.

It isn't confidence that comes first, but taking action. Confidence follows action. You do it first and then the confidence comes. We act first and then experience courage later.

The Path to Reinvention

Reinventing yourself takes time. Although change can happen instantly, consistent change that takes place over an extended period of time will have a lasting effect that sticks. In the end, we want habits and rituals that stick after the transformation takes place.

This book is one of the pathways to that reinvention. When I look back on my life and I see all that I have done [and haven't yet], part of me lingers on the idea that I could have done so much more if I hadn't been afraid. Yes, staying scared and retreating from fear kills dreams. And because we don't want to face the truth of how scared we really are, the excuses and justifications come and we think:

- *Oh, I didn't want that opportunity anyway. I'll wait for the next one.*

- *Success is overrated. It's better to stay average and not push yourself too far.*
- *The chances of making it in that competition are too low; I am not going to try something I'm sure to fail.*

Making excuses and coming up with reasons to fail are the biggest reason people don't empower themselves to take immediate action when scared. Instead, we stay scared and settle for the life that *is* instead of the life that *could be.*

As a result, we grow into a lifestyle that is waiting to deliver emotional pain in the form of regret. This is:

- The pain of knowing what you could have become if you had the courage to do the things that scared you.
- The pain of doing work you hate instead of work you love.
- The pain of making friends with people who support your life of average mediocrity because they too are scared.

The lies we tell ourselves come at a heavy price. You are paying that price a little bit every day when you stay scared and choose to do nothing. *Nothing Scares Me* is designed to get you moving toward the dreams you've buried for too long.

Consider these questions:

1. Are you where you want to be in your life today? If you answered no, would you like to be in the same place one year from now?
2. Did you have a vision for your life that brought you to the stage you're at right now? If not, do you have a vision for the next year? Can you clearly see where you are going and how you are going to get there?
3. Can you see yourself taking action to remove the biggest obstacle in your life today?
4. Are you terrified of doing this one thing? If so, what are you going to do to overcome this fear?

Life is an adventure to be lived, but sadly, many people are not living the life they dream of. Instead we are lost in the crowd of souls waking up and doing work we don't like because somewhere along the way we chose the easy path.

I don't know a lot but I do know this: our lives are short, and some are shorter than others. Much shorter. This is why we must appreciate every day.

You were brought into this world for a reason. Aren't you the least bit curious to know what it is? I know I am, and I try to uncover a bit of this treasure every day. I try to discover something new and do what part of me may want to resist creating more abundance in my life and the lives of others.

We all have reasons for staying scared, but this doesn't mean we have to like it. In this book, I will share strategies and case studies I have used to get over my fear of taking action.

When you run from fear, you take it with you. There's no escape. You cannot change or reinvent anything until you throw yourself over that hurdle of life.

Now, are you ready to empower your fear and take action today no matter how scared you are?

Let's do it…and change the way things are for the rest of your life.

See you on the inside.

Scott Allan

(Website URL)

Aim High for Your Vision of Impossibility

"So many of our dreams at first seem impossible, then they seem improbable, and then, when we summon the will, they soon become inevitable."

— Christopher Reeve

I believe in the power of impossibility. When someone says it can't be done I immediately think: *You are right. It can't be, not by you, and not with that attitude, but I'll give it a try.* However, as history has shown, impossibilities are only as real as the power we give them.

As Henry Ford once said, "Whether you think you can, or think you can't – you're right."

You don't have to change the world, but if you want to change yourself, your circumstances, or your current situation, you'll have to develop the habit of doing things that scare you.

This isn't as hard as it sounds. In fact, if you look back on your life I'm sure you'll find lots of times when you took a chance and did something when you were full of fear. You knew at that time that it had to be done no matter the outcome. You knew that pushing forward was the only way.

When we intentionally invite fear into our lives, it creates a level of discomfort that many of us are not used to. When you trust in what seems impossible, even when it pushes your current limiting beliefs, you are laying the foundation for a life of impossible dreams and circumstances.

Take a look around. Do you know someone who has created the life you crave by pushing their courage to do something most people would consider an impossibility? All successful people I know have a small band of supporters on one side and doubters on the other. People who live in fear are fearful of watching others succeed. If the impossible can be accomplished, it proves that our excuses are no longer valid.

When we no longer hold onto an excuse to validate why we can't do something, it opens the doors of possibility. Anything can be accomplished. We can break through any barrier and overcome adversity.

People who dream about success but do not take action are only dreamers. They spend their lives admiring what others have achieved and, this fills them with envy for what they could have had.

You have two choices: you can dream about it and do nothing to make it happen. Or, you can make it happen by doing something about it and then start to live your dream.

Crafting a vision and executing a plan is the best way to get to where you want to be. A life without a vision will rarely move beyond mediocre. If we stay within mediocre boundaries, we risk staying scared. If we stay scared, we become too paralyzed with fear to take any action.

Pushing Past Negative Self-Talk

We have all been there: you desire to be at a certain level but repeatedly tell yourself you can't get there. You want to believe but the voices of doubt and internal critics make you believe a different story.

Negative self-talk feeds us the "truth" about who we are and what we can do. But more often than not, what we believe isn't necessarily the truth. Our thoughts and internal beliefs just make it so.

But remember this: Your inner voices are not in control of your thoughts, actions, or behavior. You are.

When we listen to the negative voices that fill us with self-doubt, we believe the messages we receive. Who are we to doubt the voices in our own minds? Who are we to think so little of ourselves that we unconsciously decide to stay small by choice?

If you were to slow down right now and listen to the thoughts running through your head, you would be able to recognize the conversation that is running rampant. It sounds like a symphony of politicians arguing over the next tax increase.

Most of the time we operate on autopilot. But our thoughts turn into words and, those words create visual images. Your mind is powerful and can make you believe anything through this one-way conversation.

Who is controlling this conversation? You are. When you recognize that you are in control of your thoughts, you can take full responsibility for the outcome of events.

When these thoughts lead to negative words thrown about in anger, there is nobody else present to blame. It is just you. The mind takes over and tells you what you think you already know. But the truth is, we don't know what we don't know. So, we convince ourselves that what we believe must be true.

A mind filled with self-doubt creates a massive obstacle to maneuver around. Your doubt deepens your own limitations and beliefs about what is possible.

Most people, surprisingly, limit what they can do based on the doubts, opinions and limiting beliefs of others. When our peers, colleagues, or friends say that something isn't possible, the initial seed of doubt is planted in the mind.

We begin to question everything: *What if they are right? What if I fail and have to go back to the beginning? What if this makes me look bad? What if I don't have what it takes?*

When we fail to try, we never discover what we can really do. Our failure at not doing it becomes the obstacle. How do you know if you can't do something if you don't give it a shot? If you try you might fail, but it's better than doing nothing. The only way to know anything is to take a chance on doing it. If it doesn't work out, try it again using a different tactic.

You could be running these scenarios through your mind in thinking, "Who am I to…

- *Start my own business online?*
- *Travel around the world?*
- *Write a book?*
- *Earn one million dollars this year doing what I love?*
- *Quit my day job and pursue my life's passion?*

- *Deliver a keynote speech in front of thousands of people?*
- *Give up my compulsive addictions?*
- *Find the person I want to spend the rest of my life with?*
- *Journey to every country in the world?*
- *Win the Pulitzer Prize?*

People always doubt what they cannot do themselves. They fear what others can accomplish and what they themselves have failed to follow through on. But the people who achieve their goals and make dreams happen aren't lucky. They know what they want, they focus on how to get it, and then they charge forward and work until they succeed.

Don't let self-doubt stand in your way. Recognize it as the lie it is.

In actuality, it's not the negative influencers that plant the seeds of doubt in our minds that keep us from making our impossible dreams real. But rather, we do this to ourselves by subconsciously replaying the negative messages that keep us tied down. When you internalize their beliefs, this becomes your reality.

There are several key elements successful people have in common. It isn't genius, talent, or luck, although these factors play a role in being successful. Within the mind of every successful person there is a tenacious perseverance and the unbreakable belief that they are going to succeed no matter what.

Successful people struggle with doubt just like everyone else, but they have broken past it and keep pushing. Breaking the resistance is about doing what scares you even when you want to turn around and run the other way.

The difficult path is the journey. When you try to take shortcuts or do it easy, you will waste time doing work that doesn't matter. Hard work won't guarantee you success if you are working on the wrong things.

This is what we need to do if we are to face the fear of doing anything: **Continue to push forward** even when it's hard. When the going gets tough, you have to keep going.

People tend to get stuck when the way becomes difficult. During these times we have to reach out for help. Try to go it alone and you could isolate yourself, become frustrated and stop taking any risks at all. You might miss out on that opportunity or once-in-a-lifetime chance by doing it alone.

Let's take a look at Jim Carrey's story…

Years before he received a twenty-million-dollar paycheck for the movie *The Cable Guy*, Jim Carrey was doing stand-up comedy and working odd jobs to survive. But, he knew what he wanted. In fact, he was so sure of himself and his dream that he wrote a check to himself for ten million dollars and put it in his wallet.

Jim said he would walk around with it and visualize his life as a successful, highly paid actor. Several years later, Jim Carrey was holding a check for seven million dollars that he earned for *Dumb and Dumber*. Then he was paid twenty million for *The Cable Guy*. When Jim Carrey's father passed away, he slipped the check into the coffin to be buried.

Now, you might be thinking: *I don't have Jim Carrey's talent.* No, maybe you don't. He is Jim Carrey. You are you, and what you have, belongs to you. This makes you unique. Your talents, abilities, and gifts are unique. If you don't know what they are yet, that's okay. Keep searching. This takes time and there are no shortcuts.

But what you can do is imagine the impossible. See your life as it could be in five years. Put yourself in the future, visualize what you will be doing, and imagine how happy you are to be where you are.

Then, come back to the present and write down a series of action plans and tasks to get yourself there. This is how you overcome the tough obstacles in your way. When you know what you want, taking on fear and **taking intentional action** ceases to be a problem and becomes part of the process.

But, for your impossible dream to come true, you have to do two things:

1. **Be willing to do the things that scare you.** What is holding you back? What do you resist? What do you believe in? Are you repeating negative self-talk that keeps you stuck in a rut?

2. **Execute your plan.** It takes work, perseverance, and a plan to make your dream come true. What action steps can you take right now? How can you make your time more productive? Do you deal with action paralysis? What doubts stop you from moving forward?

Making Your Impossible Dreams a Reality

Take a moment to think about all the cool inventions, gadgets, and technology we have today. For a small fee, you can fly to places around the world and visit exotic locations. At the push of a button, you can instantly connect with an old friend who lives thousands of miles away. Grab a set of keys and you can drive to another state in just a few hours.

It seems like, in today's world, nothing is impossible. And yet, just one hundred years ago people could never have imagined what is possible today. It took the courage of some brave men and women to blaze the trail for the world.

As we think about the impossible possibilities that exist and surround us today, is it realistic to have limitations? Don't they exist only in our minds? If a young engineer can design an app that changes the world, why isn't anything possible? Yet, many people are scared to do what they want to do for fear of…

Failing. Yes, failure is part of the journey. It isn't something we should avoid but embrace. Most people would rather stay stuck in a job they hate for a paycheck than face the failure of doing something different.

Someone I know once said to me: "Whatever dreams I had ended when I settled for the comfort of reality."

I don't know about you but reality for me is doing what I have always been frightened to do. When you take action and do the things that our minds are telling us not to do because it is too risky, that is a signal that you are being held back.

There are many times we are challenged to do more than is expected. Watch for these opportunities and don't let them get away.

The fear of failure keeps us from pursuing our impossible dreams. Yet, great men and woman for centuries have challenged the impossible and did exactly what they set out to achieve. It doesn't matter if you're training for the Olympics, you can still do what scares you and make it happen if you want it.

If you **really** want it.

Do you want to quit your job in two years and work full time from home? You can do it if you put in the work. In two years, the impossible dream will be yours.

Do you want to create a product that helps people live better, higher-quality lives? You can do it.

How about traveling the world as a digital nomad and making a living from your online platform? It is totally possible. Rob Cubbon of http://robcubbon.com does exactly that, traveling throughout Southeast Asia while connecting with his readers through his blog, videos and online courses.

Maybe you're stuck in a painful place in your life. Maybe you want to move forward. Maybe you want to take massive action but don't know what to do. Or, maybe you want to be somebody different, but you can't let go of the person you've always been. Does it sound too good to be true?

I know, but remember that ordinary people do extraordinary things every day. They always have and always will. Someone once said to me, "All the good stuff has already been done." That's a limiting belief I don't agree with. The world always has room for another book, a new song, or a product that can improve the quality of life.

Inspire Your Passion

Colonel Sanders didn't achieve his success until he was nearly 65. For years, he tried to sell his recipe but nobody was interested. Now there are over 20,000 Kentucky Fried Chicken restaurants in 125 countries and territories around the world.

Author **JK Rowling** had the idea for Harry Potter while delayed on a train. She spent the next five years planning out the seven books of the series. JK Rowling was broke and nearly homeless by the time a publisher finally picked up the book. Relentlessly she pursued her impossible dream until it came true. Now over 400 million copies of the Harry Potter books have been sold worldwide, making her the first author to reach billionaire status.

Henry Ford had a dream to see every family in America able to afford a car. So, he created the assembly line to manufacture cars at a rate of 1,000 a day. Soon, half of the cars in the world were Fords.

Ray Kroc was a milkshake-device salesman before purchasing McDonald's at the age of 52 in 1954. He built it into the world's largest fast-food franchise, with his global vision of a McDonald's restaurant in every town and city across America.

Jerry Seinfeld was once booed offstage as a stand-up comic. He could have quit, but instead he returned to that same stage and, **tapping into the "Nothing Scares Me" mindset**, succeeded in becoming one of the most famous comedians with one of the highest ranked TV shows in history: *Seinfeld*.

It's never too late, and it's never impossible. It never has been. Impossible dreams are happening all around us. The difference between having what you want and giving up what you want is the belief that anything is possible. Only our thinking makes it real.

People who take intentional action, even when they are scared, can achieve amazing results in a short period of time. But sharing their dreams with others and being laughed at is what holds many people back.

What, you? A sport star?

What, you? A famous novelist?

What, you? Running for president?

What, you? A millionaire?

I know. I've heard it all before. Yet, these same people are living mediocre lives and doing nothing extraordinary except collecting paychecks. There is nothing impossible about that.

I've listened to naysayers most of my life. Many times I believed what they told me. It held me back for years. But I have no one to blame but myself if I do nothing to change my situation.

So, let's dream wildly, and break through our limits by smashing negative thoughts. Kick them out of your life and don't let them come back.

What Scares You That Must Be Done?

We all have dreams. Even if you aren't sure what it is yet, it is there. I don't know what yours are, but I've known mine for a long time. And I think that if you don't know what your purpose is, or you think you have nothing great to contribute to the world, you haven't dug deep enough. It's there.

You need to find it. If you don't, you risk spending the rest of your life at the mercy of someone else and their choices. In my opinion, that's the worst way to live scared -- when somebody or something decides how you should live.

Nobody chooses your path but you.

So, pull the trigger and make key choices that will impact your life for the rest of your days to come. And most importantly, choose the people who will walk it with you.

As we will see in the next chapter, the people you hang out with will either help you get to where you want to go, or they will stop you from getting there. Good company on the journey is everything.

What do you want that really scares you? In most cases, our dreams are frightening versions of a reality that we see as far, far away in another land that we can't imagine. But look at what people are doing every day. Twenty years ago, there was no social media, and now we can connect with millions of people from our own homes. Billion-dollar companies have been built and are thriving because someone had a vision and they brought it to life.

How did they do this? By believing in an impossible dream.

Did they have moments of self-doubt and fear? Certainly. But this is why we are here, to break through what holds us back, to get to where we need to be in our life. When your dream really scares you, you could be on the right path. Don't think of the fear is a warning but rather a sign that this is the way you were meant to travel.

Key Takeaways

Right now, take out a piece of paper and a pen. I want you to do a short exercise. Write down what you know to be your impossible vision of success. Whatever it is, stretch your imagination. Make it larger than life. No, bigger than that! Go large.

- If you are a writer, do you want to sell a few books, or millions of books?
- If you are working for a company, do you want to collect a paycheck, or to be the one who starts up the company of his or her dreams?
- If your passion is music, can you imagine yourself playing in front of a sold-out crowd in Las Vegas?
- Next, write down three obstacles in your life that scare you. What are they? If you can only come up with one, that is fine. Focus just on that.

- Then, write down your ideas for tackling this fear. What is the single most important step you could take right now that would get you moving towards your impossible dream?
- Now, what are you going to do scared today? Try to do just one thing that scares you. Don't wait for it to come to you. Go after it.

The Ostrich Effect and Embracing Reality

"Just as we develop our physical muscles through overcoming opposition - such as lifting weights - we develop our character muscles by overcoming challenges and adversity."

—**Stephen Covey,** author of *The 7 Habits of Highly Effective People*

The Ostrich Effect was originally coined by Galai and Sade to describe investor attempts to avoid negative financial information. When times were tough and the market was crashing, people who looked the other way and pretended everything was fine stood to risk losing their entire fortunes.

To avoid bad news or the discomfort of facing a negative situation, many people turned to entertainment devices, addictions and various methods of escapism as a means to cope. When everything was going to hell, they looked away and acted as if it would be okay.

When you bury your head in the sand to avoid the reality of a difficult situation, you risk losing everything.

If we take the Ostrich Effect and apply it to our own lives, we can spot the situations that we ignore every day. By avoiding responsibility in one area, say, for example, a bad marriage, we can avoid the discomfort of dealing with it.

By running away from reality, we can dodge a bullet and hope that we don't get hit, but it rarely works this way. Just like the investors that decide not to monitor their fortune when the market spins, we make similar choices in our own lives. These decisions can lead to emotional or financial disaster.

The Ostrich Effect is a powerful form of personal manipulative persuasion. It goes without saying that *you can run but you can't hide.* When faced with a frightening challenge, we look for someone else to carry the burden or take responsibility, and meanwhile, we create all kinds of reasons why we shouldn't take action.

Here are some examples:

When a **relationship turns toxic**, we pretend everything is okay. If we just keep our heads down and don't rock the boat, things will improve. You're in a relationship that has turned emotionally abusive, but you stick with it, telling yourself it'll get better. The worse it gets, the harder you try to pretend it will work out.

When we are **thousands of dollars in debt**, and can barely pay the monthly minimum on our credit cards, we pretend the problem doesn't exist and keep on spending. You are in debt, you have no money, and the bank is calling. You turn off your phone and head out for one last shopping spree. Months later you are bankrupt and wondering what happened.

When our **health is on the line** and the doctor has warned us of the inherent danger of smoking, we keep on doing it, ignoring the warning signs of illness. We are overweight and the doctor warned us of the health risks. Yet, we continue to shovel in the junk food and stick with a fast food diet.

Each of these situations looks and feels hopeless. You may experience one or all of these. But there are choices we can make to deal with the massive obstacles that hold us back.

You have to be ready to see the obstacles for what they are. You have to want to change and face the reality of what is happening. Only by confronting your fears can they be removed.

The Stockdale Paradox

James Stockdale was a United States Vice Admiral who was shot down in 1965 and held as a prisoner of war in Vietnam for over seven years. While captive he was routinely tortured and made to undergo some of the harshest treatments any person could endure.

When asked how he made it through alive, while other prisoners around him died, Stockdale said:

"Oh, that's easy, the optimists. Oh, they were the ones who said, 'We're going to be out by Christmas.' And Christmas would come, and Christmas would go. Then they'd say, 'We're going to be out by Easter.' And Easter would come, and Easter would go. And then Thanksgiving, and then it would be Christmas again. And they died of a broken heart."

It goes without saying that confronting the brutal facts of your reality, no matter how terrifying, is smarter that convincing yourself it is all okay when in your heart you know it really isn't.

So why do so many of us hide from the truth? Why do we choose a path of living in fear instead of confronting reality?

Jim Collins, the bestselling author of *Good to Great*, interviewed James Stockdale who went on to say:

"It comes down to faith: knowing that no matter what, you will make it through to the other side. Nobody can promise that you'll win or come out okay. You might lose everything. It is having the faith that you are strong enough to get through the worst parts of your life, whatever it may be, and that you will prevail in the end. This can only happen when you face the most brutal facts of your current reality."

Reading the story of James Stockdale, a man who had nothing left but the iron will of his own faith and a solid belief he would prevail no matter what, sets a new precedent for how we should handle impossible situations.

If James Stockdale made it through the worst hell imaginable and maintained an unbreakable faith that he would survive no matter what, what is to stop the rest of us from overcoming insurmountable difficulties?

Viktor Frankl

In a similar situation, many years earlier in October 1944 during World War II, a man named Viktor Frankl was sent to the Auschwitz concentration camp. During his imprisonment, Frankl observed death as part of daily life. He watched men succumb to their fate, often at his own feet.

In his book, *Man's Search for Meaning,* Viktor E. Frankl describes his experience in the camps, how he confronted the horrors of those days, and more importantly, how he survived:

"The experiences of camp life show that man does have a choice of action. There were always choices to make. Every day, every hour, offered the opportunity to make a decision, a decision which determined whether you would or would not submit to those powers which threatened to rob you of your very self, your inner freedom."

Therein lies the solution to either living like an ostrich or facing life with the courage of a lion; you think you have no choice, but that is a lie. You always have a choice, regardless of your current situation, in how you respond and, more importantly, how you take action.

What will you do when faced with adversity? Will you search inside yourself to discover your faith that everything will work out no matter what happens? Or will you doom yourself to a fate of hopelessness and just accept whatever comes your way by default?

Facing the reality of our current situation certainly is not easy. In the most extreme of conditions, such as the stories I just mentioned, it is life or death.

In our day-to-day life, we are forced to make decisions we don't want to make that often involve sacrifice, loss, or heartbreak. We want to procrastinate and put them off until tomorrow. We're tempted to keep busy doing other things that matter less to avoid the big issues pressing down on our lives now.

Every day we can be faced with situations that are hard, challenging, scary, or down-right terrifying. You might be going through a divorce, bankruptcy, or have recently lost a loved one. Most of us, if we are honest with ourselves, don't want to face the brutal reality of what is happening, and so we tell ourselves little lies.

These little lies come at a price: they keep you trapped. Before you realize what is happening, the situation is beyond your control. In **Nothing Scares Me**, we stand up to what scares us, no matter how bad it may be. We want to develop a faith that is unbreakable. We want to believe that no matter what, we can get through this and that we can handle whatever comes.

Here are some of the lies we tell ourselves that, as much as we would like to believe them, will bring us more pain in the long run:

- It'll work out somehow. [Reality: In other words, if I do nothing, some miracle will occur and someone will pay off my crushing debt].
- If I do nothing, somebody else will take care of it. [Reality: I created this situation, but by pretending it doesn't exist, I control my fear].
- The situation isn't as bad as I think. [Reality: It's usually worse].
- I'll fake it until I make it. [Reality: most people don't make it].

When we take the ostrich approach, like pretending that it's not as bad as we think, we are putting our lives in someone else's hands. That is a dangerous move to make. Putting your life into the hands of forces you cannot control is not a strategic plan. If you are not in control of your life and making intentional decisions about how you should be living, somebody else is.

Remember, nobody has your best interests at heart more than you do. The only guarantee you have is to put your life in good hands: your own. If, for whatever reason, you don't trust your own decision-making skills, your emotional state is fragile, or you're lacking confidence, I suggest finding someone, such as a good friend or mentor, to help you.

3 Steps to Building Rock-Solid Faith in Your Future

Make Your Commitment. Decide what you are committed to achieving and then work towards fulfilling that goal. People lose faith when they have nothing to strive for or look forward to having, being, or doing. A life without a future is dim and you will lose hope.

Stay Grounded in Reality. We can lose sight of our own reality when illusion and fantasy take over. This happens when we view reality as suffering. Let's face it: nobody wants to go through emotional trauma or suffer needlessly. But life is full of hard times. Relationships, careers, and health are always transforming. Nothing stays the same.

We lose our sense of reality when we pretend everything is okay without doing anything about it. You have to get realistic about your situation. This empowers your faith that, no matter what, this situation will pass.

Everything passes eventually. Nothing stays the same. Condition your mind to stay focused on the reality of your current state and be aware of what is happening, not what you think it should be. Then…

Reflect on Past Difficulties. What situations have you struggled with, but survived, in the past? Take a trip back through time and remember these events. Do you remember how you felt at the time? Did you think it would never end?

It's a common misperception that times of difficulty will last forever. You think to yourself: *I'll never get through this.* But you do. Take note of the stuff you've gone through that is now behind you.

By reflecting on past triumphs, we can discover faith that everything, no matter how bad it really is or seems, can be overcome. We will prevail in the end.

Key Takeaways

It is time to get realistic about the reality of your situation.

What you avoid will never go away. What we hide from eventually finds us. You end up missing out on opportunity, losing valuable relationships, or, holding onto things that tear us down when we fail to recognize them.

Are you avoiding a bad marriage, confronting a bad investment, or a situation at work that continues to get worse?

When we turn away from reality, we invite a life of fantasy and illusion. Is there an illusion you are stuck in? What are you avoiding that needs to be done? Is there anything you've been putting off? If so, why? Identifying the reason why you are avoiding something takes away its power. It gives you opportunity to create a solution.

Make a commitment to confronting your fear. Stay grounded in the reality of your situation. When things go bad, ask yourself how you can handle the situation. What are you *not* doing that could shift the outcome?

Remind yourself what your strengths are and tap into your power by focusing on this. The situation, no matter how bad it may be, only grows worse when you pretend it's not there.

Taking the First Leap from Ground Zero

Several years ago, I returned to Canada with my nine-year-old daughter for a two-week vacation. On this trip, I had an experience that changed everything, including the way I look at doing things even when I'm scared.

One day we set out to for a zip line tree adventure park. I don't know much about zip lining, but I was about to find out. After arriving we were quickly harnessed up, given a few instructions on how to use the equipment, and sent out for the adventure of a lifetime.

Just for the record, **I'm terrified of heights**.

We stayed mostly on the junior courses, practicing our zip lining no more than ten feet off the ground, which I was comfortable with. Looking through the forest at the other courses, I could see some of the other adventurers zip lining over open chasms with hundred foot drops. That was okay for them; I had no plans for that.

When my daughter became more confident, she chose to do the next level on the junior course. But while getting to the top of the first tree she had second thoughts and came back down. However, I was determined to show her it could be done. My exact words were: "You have to believe you can do it, even when you're scared."

I walked a tightrope, stepped across boards on a suspension bridge that moved constantly beneath my feet, and then swung from tree to tree on a rope thirty feet above the ground, and I made it nearly all the way to the end.

I have to admit that my fear of heights was being challenged, but not until the last part of the course. Before I continue with the story, I need to mention a few things about the rules. One is that if you run into trouble on the course, you have to yell for help. Then, a qualified instructor will come get you out of the tree.

The second rule is that if you yell for help more than three times, you will have to wear an orange hat that signals to the other instructors [and the other people on the course] that you need to be watched carefully.

I didn't want the orange hat.

At the end of the course was an eighty-foot zip line cable that crossed over a sixty-foot open chasm. I wasn't expecting that. My first instinct was to run. I looked for an emergency ladder down. Nothing. I tried to unhook both hooks and climb down when no one was looking. But we're not able to unhook both hooks at the same time. One is always permanently attached to the rope wire. In other words, I had two choices: jump, or yell for help.

Just Jump and Trust It Will Be Okay.

Two choices: do it or don't do it. We need to try at the very least to try at the challenges that stand before us. You might be scared to leap, but it's the moment before you jump that is the most frightening. Once you fully commit to going all out, your momentum will carry you the rest of the way.

I'll admit I was panicked. Fearing heights and suddenly finding myself in a situation that left me with no other choice but to take action. My daughter was on the ground looking up telling me to just "jump and get on with it." My legs were like rubber.

This is what fear does to you. It puts things in perspective. What I realized in that moment was that no matter how safe we feel, it is the safety zone of our little world that keeps us the most scared. I was no longer confident or courageous.

I was just scared. What if I jumped and something happened? What if I didn't jump and they had to pull me off the tree? Then another thought came to me: *what would happen if I jumped and made it to the other side? How would that feel?*

That is what I focused on. The *after* feeling of having succeeded. Up to that point I was focused on the worst-case scenario such as an accident, getting stuck halfway, or worse: Wearing that orange hat I could already see a couple other people walking around on the course with.

So, I just said, "To hell with it!" I leaped into open air and the world went with me. I zipped along, over the treetops, my feet dangling in open air and the feeling of nothing but empty space beneath me. I realized that a lot could change in a few seconds. Just moments ago, I was scared out of my mind, then I was doing the thing that scared me, and finally, in the end as my feet touched land, I knew I'd done it.

I did what I was afraid to do; the first few seconds were the worst. After that I was challenging what scared me the most. In reaching the other side, I had proven that being scared is okay. What you decide is going to determine how far you can go. If I had walked off the platform I would never have known. Later that day I found myself zip lining over larger valleys with drops of up to one hundred feet. I felt some tension but nothing like the scare I had on that first jump.

The **first jump** was the key. None of it would have been possible if I hadn't taken that first leap.

In life, this can go for anything such as taking up a new sport, writing a book for the first time, or starting a new relationship. If you back out before you begin, you'll always look back and think: *where would I be if only I had…?*

Now, you can apply this to any situation that scares you. Whatever you are afraid of doing in the moment can be overcome in a moment of decision. One action leads to another action. Your success in one area leads to greater success in other things.

For example:

- You want to start a new business, but you don't know where to begin? Start with the easiest step and move forward.

- You want to ask someone out on a date, but you're afraid they'll say no? Not asking them out will guarantee failure.

- You want to take an examination to get a certification in a new field of work but 90 percent of test takers fail? Go ahead and take it. What's the worst that can happen? It's better to be one of the 90 percent that failed than the 100 percent who never tried.

If we fail to take action to achieve the things we desire most, we miss out on greater opportunities down the road. You might be scared to try something now, but how will you feel if somebody else beats you to it and they succeed where you could have?

This is why, even when you're scared, you always have a choice: you can jump off the ledge or go home. If you are struggling to make the leap, just think about making it to the other side. Every time you jump, your confidence level moves up a notch.

When you back down and decide to do it next time, you face the risk of watching someone else do what you could have done, receiving what could have been yours, and living with greater confidence because of it.

Never give up your right to succeed. If you give up enough times, eventually you'll build up enough regret to last a lifetime.

Regret is painful. I know. There are many times I didn't act and now, years later, I wish had. But the past can't be changed so don't waste time focusing on what you didn't do, but on what you can and will do.

Succeeding at whatever it is you are going after, requires more than just determination or motivation. We are diving deeper than that. The people who succeed are just as scared to take action as anyone. But there is one difference: Scared people do it anyway.

They do it because they know that the fear is not going anywhere. You can't wait for courage to show up. That comes later on after you have taken action. Those that wait end up stalling and stay stuck in paralysis mode. Do you want to take action today, or not at all?

Albert E.N. Grey, author of *The Common Denominator of Success*, said: "Successful people are afraid too, but the difference is, they are willing to go the extra distance, and to do what others are afraid to do."

Susan Jeffers, the international bestselling author of _Feel the Fear and Do It Anyway_, said: "Remember that underlying all our fears is a lack of trust in ourselves."

This attitude makes a massive difference in the way we approach fear. When we feel fear, we make choices in the moment that decide the fate of everything. We choose to take action or not. You either want it or you don't. You can let yourself run away, or you can face the unknown and charge ahead.

We are surrounded by people doing things scared and succeeding. By recognizing what scares you, why it scares you, and what you are going to do about it, you become empowered to take on any challenge. Everything is difficult the first time. For many people it is easier to stay in our safe zones and avoid doing the scary stuff.

In many cases, we function from day to day without stopping to ask why? Why am I scared? Why do I give in to resistance every time? Why is everything such a struggle?

The struggle is the way. When we can push through the problems that keep us awake at night, and choose to fight as opposed to accepting the situation, we create the changes we want. Nothing happens unless you make it happen first.

Creating momentum requires force, and the strength of this force depends on your ability to take massive action and the intensity level of this action.

Creating Your 'Nothing Scares Me' Action List

After doing the things I was afraid of doing, and facing those situations I didn't want to deal with, I made a list of everything that scared me. I had forty-seven items that ranged from dealing with addictions to money issues and relationships.

As it turns out, I had a lot of "scared" issues I wasn't dealing with, and when I made a list of them I had this incredible feeling of relief, as if a part of me had been set free. I was tired of letting this fear stop me from living the way I wanted to.

While it's okay to be scared, allowing this fear to become an obstacle stopping me from taking massive action wasn't an option. So, I set out to tackle these issues and to live a scared-free lifestyle.

Action Plan

Your action plan now is to make your own list of 'scared' items you are afraid of. This can be anything from the fear of having a serious conversation with someone to paying your overdue credit card bill.

Set aside thirty minutes. Then, list out all the things you have been avoiding or are afraid of doing. This can involve anything from personal relationships to career moves. Just make a list of the challenges you know is holding you back. Whatever you resist should be on the list.

Here are a few of the items I had on my list:

- Interacting with people in a social environment.
- Going to the bank to pay a bill that was months overdue.
- Having that "talk" with my daughter.
- Asking for more time off work.
- Creating a yearly financial savings plan.
- Making an appointment with the doctor for that much needed health check.
- Resigning from my current job and pursuing a new profession.

After making your list, prioritize it from top to bottom. Ask yourself: *what can be done right now?* If there is anything that can be taken care of quickly, do it today. By crossing something off your list you'll get a boost of confidence and that makes it easier to move onto the next item.

For bigger items you can create an extensive list of mini action steps. For example, one of the things on my list was setting up a monthly savings plan, but this required multiple action steps. Feeling overwhelmed, I had to break it down into manageable chunks. By breaking it into several smaller steps, I was able to get it done.

We resist taking action towards our goal at times because we are afraid we will fail at achieving them. You might fail if you try, but you'll certainly fail if you don't.

So go ahead. Write down all of the obstacles, challenges and fears that are keeping you stuck today. Keep going until you have exhausted all of your ideas. By the time you are done, you'll have a list of unfinished tasks to get to work on.

The key is to take them one by one. Break each task down into smaller steps. Focus on the details of each one. By completing the work that has gone unfinished, you can push through the shame and fear of living with failure.

Key Takeaways

Your safety zone is a place of comfort that can keep you stuck. We have to commit to a goal that is larger than we are to break free from this zone.

We resist taking action towards our goals because we are afraid of failing to achieve them. What are you resisting right now?

What massive action steps could you take today to start building momentum? What is your current goal, and what action steps are you taking to accomplish your milestone?

We have a choice in every difficult situation. What choices are you making right now?

Do you know what scares you? Make a list of your fears. Then, next to each fear, write down an action step you are taking to overcome this fear.

The first jump is always the most frightening. What is your first leap going to be?

Partnering With the Right People

> *"If your emotional abilities aren't in hand, if you don't have self-awareness, if you are not able to manage your distressing emotions, if you can't have empathy and have effective relationships, then no matter how smart you are, you are not going to get very far."*

— Daniel Goleman

There is a saying about the company you keep: "If you hang out with five idiots, you are the sixth idiot."

If you spend your time with five successful entrepreneurs, you are the sixth. Spend your time with five productivity gurus whose focus is on getting things done, you're the six. Spend your time with five complainers, and you're the sixth complainer.

You can tell a lot about someone by the company they keep, both in their personal lives and in their professional lives.

We subconsciously gravitate toward the crowd that fits into our version of reality. As we choose our crowds, we make choices about our destiny by choosing the people who will help to shape it. The person you become is in alignment with the people you attract and spend the most time with.

Take a look around you at the people you associate with every day. Do you talk like them? Think like them? Do you look up to them? This is your circle of powerful influence, and it will have a profound impact on your success or failure in the coming years.

My grandfather once said to me, "You'll only reach the summit of the tallest mountain if you are climbing with the right people." There is no point in reaching for the top if the people around you are holding you back.

The people you hang out with are not just a reflection of your thinking and mindset; they are contributing to it. The person you associate with and spend the most time with measures your success.

When it comes to reaching your goals and objectives, the people you are in direct contact with will either help you get there, or hold you back. So choose wisely when you build your team.

They are your warriors on this journey. You will need them when the going gets tough.

This is why, when taking on challenges that scare you, it is easier to go through the experience surrounded by people who are doing it too. Wouldn't you rather spend time with someone who is encouraging you to take action, rather than someone who habitually procrastinates?

Scared people who stay scared rarely do anything to change. They are too afraid to. And, the people who hang around with them often share a similar mindset. If you want to win, you have to stick with the people who are winning.

Four Strategies for Building Better Connections

1. Join a Mastermind Group

One of the best things I ever did was hook up with several mastermind groups online. Depending on what you are into, there are groups for just about any level of support these days. If you are finding it hard to partner up with the right people in your area, start with some online connections. It isn't the same as meeting up with someone for coffee, but you can chat in real-time and join live webinars.

A mastermind group is made up of people with similar interests. You can work toward goals, key objectives, and even start a business with online connections.

Nobody can make it alone. We need support, encouragement, and positive interaction with good people. Better yet, you can do things you'd normally put off with someone else. It is always easier if you are in the company of friends.

People partner up to take on projects, create businesses, or work on new innovations together. A solid partnership can make the difference between **doing it NOW**, and not doing it at all.

In the last ten years, social media has provided us with relationships that span the globe. We can connect through chats, video, or audio. There are very few boundaries these days. It is amazing. While we shouldn't rely entirely on online friends for support, there are times when we have to connect with people, the right people, wherever they may be. This is, in fact, how I continue to build my online platform.

2. Avoid the Scared People Who Spread Fear

We can find the people who support our mission by, first of all, letting go of the people who don't. Before we set out to find these people, we should take a look at the crowd in our lives and ask: *Will these people work with or against me? Are we working towards a common goal, or not?*

A friend of mine, who realized his dream after working in the wrong profession for nearly ten years, had surrounded himself with people who didn't support his goals. After carefully analyzing the situation, he gradually let people go by reducing the amount of time he spent with each of them. When he was ready to move on, nobody cared because he had created a totally new group of friends that shared a common interest in his new path.

People who live in fear and take no action will spread that fear to everyone they meet.

Their fear becomes a contagious virus and we should stay away from them. They'll eventually find their own crowd of haters.

What I've seen happen in several relationships is that the man or woman suddenly realizes they have a mission to fulfill. This could be a dream that must be recognized, a life purpose discovered, or something even greater.

As they become aware and try to share this newfound discovery with their partners, they are met with disappointment and resistance. The partner or spouse has a different agenda and isn't interested in the other person's new way of life.

I am not suggesting you walk away from all your relationships to live the life you've always dreamed of, but in many cases, this is what happens. We try to involve those in our lives at that time, but sometimes we come to realize, it's like trying to fit a round peg into a square hole. I've seen others do the opposite as well where instead of breaking free, they opt in to stick with their crowd and stay scared like the rest of them.

If you are partnered up with someone in your professional or personal life whose relationship is causing pain and stress, consider your options. Look for an exit strategy. Get out. Make it your mission to find the right crowd of people, because they are out there. But you'll struggle to connect with them if your mind set is elsewhere.

The scope of this book doesn't include walking you through major relationship shifts, but if you recognize your situation needs to be changed, you'll be the one to change it. Don't let toxicity ruin your chances of living a remarkable life. The wrong people can hold you back from your journey. The right people will help you get there.

3. Stick with Your Influencers

The people in your life not only influence your actions, but also your state of mind and attitude. The people you are with feed directly into your emotions. They impact your thoughts and affect motivation.

What you feel is how you act. If you are charged up emotionally and surrounded by positive people, there is no limit to what you can do. But hang with the naysayers who don't believe you can do it, tell you you're crazy or that what you are planning is impossible, and you'll start to act like it.

Connect with people who exchange ideas and are in it with you to further the quality of both your lives. If you can only connect with people online, that is better than hanging out in person with naysayers. Foster positive relationships and you'll reduce your scared factor exponentially. But stay connected to those negative relationships and you'll be afraid every waking moment.

Is there someone holding you back? Do you already have a supportive community helping you? Are you still unsure the type of crowd you need? Regardless of your situation, our goal is to create a positive community of friends, family members, and partners who can share insight, ideas and a common vision. If the right people are with you for the journey, they'll stick with you to the end.

4. Go Where Your Crowd Is

In order to discover your tribe, you have to know where they hang out and start hanging out there. **Focus** is key. Know who matters and whom you need to keep at a distance.

Emotionally disconnect from the people that are filling your mind with self-doubt. This can be tough to do if they are coworkers or family, but when we listen to the naysayers, we become one of them. It will happen without you being aware of it.

Remember that we become the model of those people in our lives. If you're not helping each other, you're most likely tearing each other and everyone else down. Know who you should focus on, and give that group or person your attention. You might be in a situation at work where you have to spend eight hours a day with people you don't like.

If this is the case, and because most people don't get to choose their coworkers, being around people you have negative feelings towards affects your mental health. It can be exhausting. You are always on guard.

A friend of mine recently went through a rough divorce after 15 years of marriage. When I asked him why he married in the first place, he said that in the beginning the relationship was a positive and healthy partnership. He felt energized by his partner, as if they were unbeatable. But, over the years, those feelings changed.

When the marriage turned toxic, and those positive emotions were replaced by contempt and negativity, it was time to get out. Eventually he separated and several years later he discovered the person of his dreams. He went on to build a successful business and turned what could have been an unhappy life into a positive event.

Without a doubt, the relationships you forge do matter.

A good relationship will make you; a bad one will break you. When you are showing up every day and the people around you are creating a fear-based, paralyzing environment, you have to change it, put up with it, or become a victim of circumstances.

Key Takeaways

- Find people who support, encourage, and believe in you. Reduce the amount of time and increase the amount of distance between you and the people who steal your energy. Naysayers are not welcome.
- Identify the relationships in your life that do you harm. These can be toxic and unhealthy to your success. Worse yet, they promote fear and

are keeping you from acting. Then, look for ways to break away and reduce the amount of proximity time.

- Stay active and hook up with the right people. They are out there, but you'll have to find them. Know the kind of people you want to forge partnerships with. Follow them online, send them messages, or make plans to meet. Model what they are doing and ask lots of questions.
- Emulate the kind of success you want and hang out with the right people who are committed to continuous support and encouragement.

At the Risk of Looking Stupid

"Fearlessness is not only possible, it is the ultimate joy. When you touch nonfear, you are free."

— Thich Nhat Hanh

The #1 obstacle that stands between us and doing it scared is the fear of failing and looking like a fool.

We all know that feeling. Everyone is watching you. Some are waiting for you to make a mistake or fail so they can make an example out of you. Now, your boss at work just handed you a project on a subject you know little about.

Your initial thoughts are:

What if I screw up? What if I look incompetent? I'll lose face in front of everyone and then I'll have to look for another job. But what if it happens again at the next job? When will I stop feeling this way?

The fear of taking action leads to inaction. The fear of looking stupid triggers avoidance mechanisms and you go into paralysis mode. You look for a way out, a way to escape. People who are afraid of looking dumb often judge others when they screw up.

Risk is an opportunity to fail. You avoid putting yourself out there because, somewhere along the way, you've adopted a set of limiting beliefs that are keeping you trapped. Risking anything by taking a chance on a new idea, venture, or relationship, feeds into our fear of rejection. People who are afraid of being rejected, and have instilled that fear as a kind of phobia, are masters of avoiding risky situations.

Here are some examples:

- You don't ask someone out because you think they'll say NO and you'll look like a fool.
- You don't apply for that job you want because you think there will be tons of applicants and you'll look stupid going up against such tough competition.
- You don't start that book because you think you suck as a writer. So why humiliate yourself by having people read your bad writing?
- You don't voice your opinion during a conversation because you think you might say the wrong thing and, once again, sound like an idiot.

It's true that there is risk in taking chances. People who are overly sensitive and shy will be affected more than those that charge full speed ahead. The difference is, those charging ahead are probably afraid too, but they are willing to take a chance to find what lies beyond their fear.

This is a powerful lesson we can learn from. We spend so much time and effort avoiding what we are scared of because we don't want to face the humiliation of making a mistake. But, when we don't put ourselves out there, we make no progress. We stay the same. We stay stuck.

In sixth grade, I was terrified of playing baseball. It is, perhaps, the only sport I can say I hate more than anything. I know, it is loved by millions of fans and one of the most popular sports in both the US and Japan, but when I was growing up, playing baseball was the same as looking like a complete fool. Here is why.

When I was up to bat, I would strike out nine times out of ten. Perfect pitches came across the plate and I would still miss the ball entirely. When I was in the outfield and the ball came my way, I'd fumble it almost every time.

I could neither catch nor hit. In other words, not only was I the worst player on the team, but also,

I'd get taunted by the other players for never being able to hit or catch the ball.

Baseball just wasn't my sport. I developed a fear of playing because I was tired of looking stupid. The other players, even the ones on my own team, laughed whenever I stepped up to the plate, struck out, or missed a fly ball. It was embarrassing.

I learned to dislike the sport because it instilled in me a fear of looking dumb. It sapped my confidence, and I left my self-esteem at the plate every time.

There are many other examples of things I've failed at. My performance in school was weak, and most years I would barely scrape by with passing grades. Over time, I identified myself as someone who wasn't smart or successful. Gradually, I stopped taking risks or striving for what I wanted. My fear of failing had instilled in me a belief that it was better to not try and put myself on the spot than do it and end up looking bad.

Why Looking Stupid Is So Shameful

The alternative to doing it scared is living with shame. After a lifetime of failing or looking bad, we learn to cover up what we don't want the world to see. We all have weak spots, and to protect ourselves we hide these weaknesses from everyone, including ourselves.

We learn at a young age to avoid failing. Like not being able to hit a ball in the big game, we don't want to be singled out as the one who isn't going to make it. So instead we try to blend in, play by the rules, and do just enough to not get noticed for playing bad or well.

You want to ask someone out on a date, but if he or she says no, you are left with that feeling of rejection and it validates your sense of low esteem. So we avoid the risks and stay below the radar. But that is not the place success thrives.

We can only be confident when we act with confidence, regardless of the outcome. When I was trying to hit a ball and I couldn't, it didn't matter. I was at the plate and trying to smash a home run. When others laughed, it didn't matter because with every swing, I got closer to that big play.

Just as in baseball, in life you need to step up to the plate and take your turn at bat. If you strike out, it doesn't mean you'll fail at everything. But you will if you say no to everything. It's okay to miss your shot, whether it be in sports or failing a job interview.

Becoming Fearless

Gary Vaynerchuck is one of my favorite speakers. As the founder of the #AskGaryVee Show, he is a prolific entrepreneur, author, and Internet personality.

But what I like most about him is his fearlessness. Gary tells it how it is and he doesn't sugar coat anything.

Gary has delivered keynote speeches to millions of people. He is direct, straightforward, and honest. He shows us that we can do whatever we want to do if we can get over that fear of failing.

As Gary says:

"If I said one of the hardest things about making your dream, or your small business, or your blog, or whatever, happen was just *doing it*, would you believe me? Because the truth is, that *is* the hardest part. And ironically, that is the one big thing standing in your way. Just executing. Nobody can argue with execution. Once you're getting shit done, you're on your way."

You might be scared, putting it off, avoiding what needs to be done, but once you do something, you're triggered to charge forward. You become fearless by pushing through the fear and doing what scares you. If you're waiting for permission to take action, give yourself permission. Be fearless by looking at your fear through the other end of the scope.

Think of it this way. You're going to die someday. Do you want to look back with regret on the things you ran away from? Do you want to be one of those people who dies knowing you could have been larger than life and serving a life greater than your own? You have this life to charge forward and do your thing.

How to Evaluate a Win-Win Situation

Where would you be without mistakes? Can you remember the last time you made a big mistake? How did you feel or react? Did you take responsibility?

I once worked with someone who blamed all his mistakes on everyone else. No matter what happened, it was someone else's fault, even when it clearly wasn't. This person also lived with a lot of fear, pointing his finger or denying that he'd done anything wrong at all. He was so scared of the world that he never interacted with others or made friends, either at work or outside of it.

This person was always on edge, looking out for himself, never trying anything different or challenging because he feared screwing it up. When the company shifted gears and needed people who could think innovatively, he didn't make the team. The world needs more people who are ready to take action when scared and not run away from fear.

But fear affects all of us differently. You could be a perfectly rational human being and then, when put into a situation that threatens your security, start to lie, cheat, and act in a way that suggests you've been taken over by aliens.

A mentor of mine used a unique approach. He would look at each day as a new opportunity to grow, do something different, and embrace the time he had. He was honest and laughed at his own mistakes, and he made more mistakes than anyone. Why? Because he tried so many new things. It didn't matter if it was related to a tech issue he knew nothing about, or taking on a new role he wasn't prepared for.

When a challenge presented itself, he would take it. When he wasn't asked, he volunteered. You see, many people avoid being selected for new things. They would rather hide in the shadows and hope that somebody else gets picked. But that's not how we get better.

What stops many people from taking action is the fear of losing what they have. But what do we really have if what we hold isn't what we want? How can we call ourselves wealthy when we live in fear of scarcity? What will happen if you take that risk and succeed?

The fear of looking like a fool is related to low self-esteem and perfectionism. You are worried about what the people will think. Great achievements are made when people put themselves out there and take chances. By not doing anything, you are denying yourself the opportunity to be great. You don't want to be great? You're not reading this book because you love mediocrity.

You believe in the possibility that you can cultivate a life that is more than just ordinary. There is nothing wrong with ordinary either, but let's face it, who doesn't want to do something extraordinary at least once in their lives?

We all have a gift and ability to do something brilliant with our lives. Find out what it is and make it happen.

Key Takeaways

- Reflect on a time when you did something without worrying about looking foolish [this should be when you were not intoxicated]. What was the result?
- Make a list of things you avoid because you fear looking foolish. It could be that you're

scared of failing in front of a group, or, looking silly just isn't your thing.

- Record a video of yourself speaking to your audience. This can be anything. You can record yourself trying to do 50 pushups every day or twenty minutes of resistance training. People love it when you share the greatest parts of yourself. You can record it and then, when you are feeling more confident, you can start up a Facebook group or YouTube channel.

Disguising Fear with Distraction

"All the adversity I've had in my life, all my troubles and obstacles, have strengthened me... You may not realize it when it happens, but a kick in the teeth may be the best thing in the world for you."

— Walt Disney

Since the Internet has radically shaped the way we live – bringing access to social media, games, and unlimited information – this generation has been accused of creating a world of productivity killing distractions. When I don't feel like doing something, I find a way to escape it.

In today's world, this is easy to do. There is no limit to the number of distractions we can use to keep our minds fixed on something else. The problem is, these distractions are set up to lead us away from working on the tasks and goals that matter.

Here is an example: you have a project that needs to be finished in three days and you've hit a rough spot. Instead of digging in and fixing the problem, you start a new project, or change gears and begin doing something completely unrelated to get your mind off of it.

You promise to get back to it first thing the next morning. But the next day you are busy doing something else. You keep finding reasons why it can't be done. Then Friday comes, you've missed the deadline, and you lose the contract with the customer.

Sounds familiar? It's happened to all of us. For some people, it has turned into an addiction. Think back to a time when you put something off because the thought of doing it created so much resistance that you couldn't deal with. This can be anything, but our need to be distracted is merely an excuse generator. You might feel busy, but are you really? Is what you are doing right now more important than what you know needs to be done?

Creating distractions has never been easier than it is in today's world. We are always just an arm's reach away from a device or remote control. We can access whatever we desire any time of the day. In other words, we are living limitless in a world with unlimited choices to keep our minds as busy [and distracted] as possible.

We all struggle with 'distraction obstacles.' Whenever I come across a problem that is challenging and that I'd rather not tackle, my first instinct is to find something else to do to divert my attention from the problem. This is what I refer to as *fear avoidance*. We avoid dealing with difficult issues by replacing them with something that is fun and easier to deal with. This is how procrastination happens.

When we avoid tough situations, like paying bills or having difficult conversations with people, we are putting off an inevitable fearful situation that isn't going to go away. As soon as we think *I can't handle this*, we'll do anything to avoid it. But what we turn a blind eye towards doesn't just disappear. Unresolved situations are stressful, and we carry the internal stress around with us wherever we go.

When situations or difficulties are unresolved, you become exhausted quicker. Your mind is working overtime to figure out a solution while you are busy trying to keep it distracted. Until we can deal with the problem and reach a resolution, we will always feel the burden of the things that are left incomplete.

Here are a few examples of tough situations that, when avoided, trigger stress:

- Unpaid bills that cause creditors to call your home.

- Avoiding a conversation with someone that leads to a misunderstanding and worsens the situation.

- Putting off finding a new job leads you to have to do more work you hate.

- Eating junk food instead of a healthy meal leads to bigger health problems and weight gain.

- Rapid life changes that disrupts the normal flow of your routine.

I get the whole *I'll take care of it later* routine. For years, I avoided every uncomfortable situation. I became a passive observer in life, and it led to more problems than I can count. Issues went unresolved, resentments built-up and turned relationships sour, and my unhappiness hit an all-time low. It became obvious to me that fear avoidance is a short-term plan that sets us up to fail.

You might escape the problem in the NOW, but you'll pay for it LATER. When we put off tasks and projects that we should do NOW, and replace them with passive activities such as watching TV or surfing the Internet without any purpose other than to kill time, we're creating bad habits that can spiral out of control.

Procrastination and the Art of Postponing Critical Work

From a young age, I learned to procrastinate and put everything off. But *later* wasn't that far in the future. In school I put off doing homework until the last minute only to rush through it when it had to be done. For years, I put off creating a financial plan only to be hit with large credit card bills and bankruptcy.

Over the course of time, I had developed the habit of saying I would *do it later.* When you buy into short-term pleasure, you are investing in long-term pain. What you focus on is eventually what you become.

Buying into short-term pleasure is investing in long-term pain. *This is the core of our fear.*

It wasn't until years later that I learned to confront my fear. When I was scared, I moved forward with a plan of action. Even a simple plan is better than nothing. The act of running away was so ingrained that it became an automatic response. If you want more freedom in your life, you need to take care of business — unfinished business.

Time management creator and productivity consultant **David Allen** calls this "Getting Things Done." This is exactly what we need to shift towards: getting the things that scare us finished. It is these obstacles we face every day that are the hardest to maneuver around.

What I propose is this: make a list of the stuff you have been avoiding. Do it now.

For example, here is a short list of what I have been avoiding:

- Talking with my wife about money issues.
- Hiring someone to design my website so I can run my online business.
- De-cluttering the house so we have more room to breathe.
- Talking with a co-worker about their unacceptable behavior.
- Starting a report that has to be finished in two days.
- Cancelling my credit card.
- Making a dental appointment.

By the time I had finished my list there were over forty things I'd been avoiding. By avoiding what needed to be done, I created a stressful lifestyle. It's like a garbage heap you keep throwing trash onto and then when it's huge, you try to cover it up. It stinks after a while until you find a new place to move it. So, get in the habit of clearing away your junk pile. Don't let it stink.

I've learned that when I trained myself, through positive habit development, to take care of business right away, I felt empowered. With everything I had to do, I was overwhelmed and took no action at all. I would always say, *I'll do it tomorrow.* Tomorrow would come and I'd get busy with something else. By keeping myself occupied with other things, I avoided doing the stuff that mattered most.

You might be forced into doing it scared, but that's nothing like the fear you'll have years later when you start to pay for the consequences of your procrastination. Do you want to pay now or later? Do you want to suffer now or even worse later? Do you want to go through a difficult period now or later?

Do it now, get the things that are holding you back done, and push through the challenges that are in your way. Start now by taking action on the one thing that scares you.

Here is a short list of the **distractors** that keep you **scared**. Can you add any more to this list?

- TV [when it is used to numb out and escape]
- Addictions
- Entertainment sources that keep us busy
- Harmful relationships
- Overeating

- Compulsive shopping
- Excessive social media interaction
- Compulsive email and texting

We can use anything to distract ourselves from the fear of reality, but is it reality or the illusion that is more frightening? Reality can be terrifying, and the world is not at a loss for activities that divert our attention when we need it.

Getting Connected with Reality

I know someone who watched TV for a month because he was afraid to deal with a painful divorce. He said that when he watched television it was like he became a device that tuned everything else out. But, when the distraction was gone, the pain returned. And, it would come back with nasty ferocity. There is nothing wrong with watching some TV, but when you over-use things as a means to escape you are setting yourself up to fail in the long term.

I know what it's like to be stuck in a situation that is terrifying to deal with. We all deal with fear differently. Going through a bad relationship, sickness, bankruptcy, or even dealing with day-to-day living can be stressful.

Remember that everything is temporary. It passes. You can get through it no matter what. The time will pass regardless, and if you decide to confront your difficulties now instead of avoiding them you'll be able to enjoy yourself later, which has so much more to offer.

When we lose the ability to cope, we distract ourselves with actions that disable our power. The things we try to avoid don't just disappear. As many recovering alcoholics have discovered when they first became sober, life is always happening even when they aren't present. The problems they avoided were usually left unattended and either became worse or, someone else had to step in and take care of it.

When we turn away from fear, we are making a conscious decision not to handle it. We are, in fact, saying no to becoming great.

When we run we make life more difficult than it has to be. Or worse, we admit that we can't handle it, and it is better left unresolved. Or, we hope that someone else steps in to do something.

As I said earlier in this book, we make two choices at the beginning of each day: either we empower ourselves to take action or, we live scared by running away from our problems and stay in hiding.

Make a choice and take a stand right now to stop running and start doing. Tackle your actions with intention.

When we take on challenges that frighten us, it increases our ability to handle any situation. We never have the chance to learn from what we avoid and run from. It's like shooting yourself in the foot. You might con yourself into thinking you're getting away with it, but this is a lie you shouldn't believe.

Reality can be frightening, but as I learned the hard way, not nearly as frightening as waking up one day and realizing you can no longer turn off the problem. You need to either fight or fail. There can be no victory when the challenges we face defeat us. You are only defeated if you make up your mind to be. It's never over until you've given up.

Key Takeaways

- Stay focused when you feel like running. Stand your ground and ask yourself: *what am I risking by not standing up to this situation?*
- Be aware of your distractors. We all have our favorite devices. Catch yourself when you are using something to zone out or escape. This is a sign you are practicing fear avoidance.

- Make a list of the things that distract you and reinforce the action habit: **Take action with intention.** Don't wait. The longer you wait, the more difficult it will be to solve the problem later. Do you want to suffer now or later? Short-term pain leads to long-term happiness.
- Everything is temporary. When we avoid the things that must be done, we are just inviting more stress into our lives. Unfinished business remains that way until you take responsibility for it.

Putting Your Self-Doubt on the Ropes

"Stop trying to be less of who you are. Let this time in your life cut you open and drain all of the things that are holding you back."

— Jennifer Elisabeth

Self-doubt is a very powerful form of fear. Robbing people of confidence, self-esteem, and creating deep-seated hopelessness, it is the #1 dream killer.

Self-doubt kills motivation and causes you to hesitate to take action. Not knowing what to do next, you become paralyzed with fear that keeps you stuck in the same repetitive cycle, even if the cycle isn't working.

Let's get focused on how to eliminate self-doubt and improve your game in life.

Why Do We Doubt Ourselves?

We all have stories of losing confidence and failing to follow through when we were scared or didn't want to deal with a situation. In times of deep fear, it's in our nature to defend ourselves, to flee and protect our fragile ego.

Many people have suffered from self-doubt for so long and from such a young age that they don't know any other way to live. In severe cases, some of us turn to introversion or build fantasies around how life should be instead of how it is.

To change, we have to stay grounded in the reality of what is happening now. But there are no shortcuts to overcoming feelings of self-doubt. It is a decision you need to make each day.

For today, you will take at least one progressive action to raise your confidence level. You will reach out to people who need help, and you will ask for help in return. You could do one thing you are resisting. You could throw out your negative thoughts and replace them with positive affirmations.

You can turn introversion and fear into extroversion and courage. It all starts with a simple action. You could implement a positive thought that pushes you to overcome a limiting belief. Or, when you are retreating into yourself and the voices of doubt fill your mind, you can recognize what is happening and try to correct it.

The key to taking control of your life is deciding what you are willing to accept and what you are not willing to accept. I, for example, refuse to allow the voices that occupy my mind to control my thoughts. If they control my thoughts, they tap into my fear. When that happens, fear takes over and I fall back into a mental prison again.

When you choose to take the *Nothing Scares Me* approach, you are holding the key to your freedom. Now you can turn the key and do something about it.

The Beliefs that Create Doubt

In the beginning of this book I told you I failed throughout most of my school years. The main reason, I realized later, was because I had built up a powerful resistance to failing. Instead of taking on new challenges, I avoided them. I distracted myself, filling my valuable time with activities I couldn't fail at: video games, television, or playing around with social media [you know, cat videos].

What is the problem with this? When you repeatedly practice habits that lead you away from your true objectives, they become your default strategy whenever *scared* moments appear.

By creating a predictable lifestyle in your comfort zone, you strengthen the walls of your mental and emotional prison. Your comfort zone is not always a bad place, but the more you stay there the less you progress.

Self-doubt is like fungus in the mind; it needs a place to grow. Unknowingly and subconsciously, many people feed into their self-doubt every minute of the day with addictions, limiting beliefs, worn-out thoughts, and out-of-control behaviors that destroy character.

When we overcome, we become greater. When we run, we are reduced to mediocre shadows of what we could be.

The First Instinct

Every moment that challenges you and every new problem you experience will scare you. That's it. With every situation, I have ever faced, from getting on an airplane for the first time, moving to a new country, starting at a new company, or meeting new people, anxiety and fear are all part of the game.

You might think there is something wrong with you if you feel afraid to give a speech, but this is perfectly normal. In fact, it is necessary. When you **take massive action** in the face of fear, you improve your game. By doing something new, you become stronger. By taking action, you build your confidence and eliminate self-doubt.

Controlling Your Fear

Several years ago I attended a conference to listen to several keynote speakers. For the record, public speaking is a terrifying experience that I struggle to overcome even today.

At this conference the speaker, who had just finished giving a speech to over one hundred people, suddenly handed the podium over to me. A minute before I had been enjoying sitting at a table, watching, and listening. There was no pressure to do anything. Suddenly, I was being asked to deliver some words to this large group without any preparation.

My first initial reaction was to leave. I wanted to run. If I had been sitting near an emergency exit I might have. I broke out in sweat. It was cold fear, and I was stuck in a spot I couldn't get out of. My colleague was holding out the mic and it took me several seconds to realize I wasn't reaching for it. Then in the process of taking it I stood up and nearly fell over. Rubbery legs. Dry throat. I knew that I had to deliver and that there was no running away. My self-doubt screamed, *this is it! You're going to crash and burn!*

I successfully delivered a short speech without panicking. I knew, in that moment, that this was how you get over the fear of doing anything: by doing it. I just relaxed and spoke as if I was speaking to an audience of friends. If I started to think about my words, or doubt that what I was saying was worthy, the panic would creep in.

Leaving perfection out of the equation is what pulled me through.

This simple practice can work for you too. We get focused on doing it right or we doubt that we aren't good enough. You might think, "If only I have another day to practice this it'll be much better." What we are doing is putting it off. This creates more anxiety. The longer you take to think it over and consider if your actions are right, the more opportunity you are giving yourself to screw it up. By the time it's game time, you are shaking so bad you'd rather be anyplace else.

You can only win the game by playing the game. The next time somebody challenges you to take action and step outside your comfort zone, accept it and thank that person right away.

I learned something powerful in those moments of fear: it can be controlled.

This is how you deal with those scared moments. You face the truth that this challenge is not a punishment, but something that will make you better, develop your character, and push you out of the comfort zone. Remember that, as you reach out and try new things, you'll always be afraid. But that scared moment is temporary. Fear doesn't last forever. You can, however, spend the rest of your life regretting the things you don't do.

Mastering Your Mind

One of the most powerful weapons you have is the mastery of your mind. Self-doubt is like an illness that attempts to rob you of this mastery. It makes you weaker by feeding into your fears.

And what do we fear most?

Confronting problems, new experiences, and the fear of failing. You are going to challenge the self-doubt in your life by challenging the negative voices in your head, the thoughts you create, and the anxiety feeding off your fearful state. This sounds like a lot to take in, but it is a formula that works.

As we question our fears, we can see the lies that exist. Self-doubt is created when our fears are made real. When we fail, it feeds our fears, but only if we believe failure is a bad thing, only when we judge ourselves too harshly or believe that all is lost. You stay scared when you think there is no way out. If you stay trapped behind closed doors, you'll never break free.

Are you ready to open those doors?

Tactics for Challenging Your Self-Doubt

I use a simple formula to challenge my fears and doubt. I know it works because I've been using it for years when I am faced with difficulty, challenges, and problems.

Challenge #1: You Will Always Have Self-doubt Until You Do Something. You can't just *think* yourself into a successful outcome. You have to take action and do the thing you're afraid of. Self-doubt, fear, and uncertainty are facts of life. We all have fears until we rise above the challenge. Take action when you're feeling self-doubt and you'll crush it every time. Avoid and run away and the doubt will stick around.

Action is powerful. It puts you in control of the situation instead of becoming a victim of circumstances. Taking action instantly boosts your confidence. It is the one solution that never fails. Provided, of course, that you are taking the right actions and doing something that brings you closer to your goals. This is the first step in creating that thriving lifestyle you are after.

The question is, what are you going to do today? Right now, write down [in pen and on paper] one action that you will take today to push back against your doubts. This can involve a current challenge you are facing, or something you've been putting off because you fear failing.

We all have these so it should be easy to choose something.

Challenge #2: Everyone Is Scared. We see people as superhuman when they get out there and do what seems impossible. But what appears impossible to many is simply an obstacle to some. Any obstacle can be removed when you decide to confront life's difficulties.

Do you think you are the only one who's scared? Is fear and self-doubt exclusive to your life? No, we all have it. Your case isn't any more special than mine. What differentiates us is how we control our fear and do what scares us even when our instincts tell us to give up.

We're all scared. But this can be used to our advantage. If you want to master your life, do the one thing that scares you the most.

Make a list of the things you are scared of. There is no shame in this. Creating the list will bring the stuff you should be aware of to light. Awareness of our fear is the first step to removing it. Make your list right now.

Challenge #3: Forge a Confident Identity. Convert your identity from someone who believes they are a failure to someone who is a true winner. Deep feelings of doubt and uncertainty can mold themselves into an identity. That is to say, we identify ourselves as people who lack confidence.

Have you ever said to someone, "I'm not a confident person"? In saying that, you act it out. Our words have power. Repeating is the same as molding ourselves into that image.

You were not born with doubt; you created it. Recognizing this helps you shift from a victim to someone who can handle anything. If you identify yourself as someone who is afraid to fail, you'll continue to fail. If you label yourself as weak or incapable of handling fearful situations, then you'll run every time something happens. By shifting your identity, you can gain greater personal power.

Self-doubt is only as strong as the power you feed it. Take away its power with positive self-talk. Replace your negative voice with powerful choice words. When you experience doubt, ask yourself: "What am I thinking or doing that makes me feel this way? How can I shift away from this thought?" By questioning the power it has on you, you take away its power and give yourself greater confidence to step up to a new level.

Avoid saying things like:

- I'm no good at this.
- I don't have the confidence to succeed.
- I don't want to fail so why bother.
- Who am I to try this?
- I don't have the talent or creativity.

Stay focused on every word spoken. What you say and how you say it fuels your desire to take action. Your words create concrete thoughts and beliefs. Your thoughts control your words and manage your confidence. Stay focused on your thoughts above all else.

Key Takeaways

- When you repeatedly practice habits that lead you away from your true objectives, they become your default strategy whenever *scared* moments appear.
- Self-doubt is the negative belief that you are incompetent, incapable, and seemingly hopelessly unable to succeed. Do you think so? Is this true? Or are you being manipulated by a lower state of mind? Is your doubt in your own character a permanent flaw, or do you believe it can be turned around?
- Everyone is scared. We all have doubts and uncertainties. What matters is how we confront these fears.
- Listen to your negative voices. What are they telling you? Do you believe the thoughts that you are creating? Focus on this self-talk and learn to talk back.
- Negative internal dialogue is your fear taking over. Create your own dialogue by turning off the negativity and replacing it with powerful words that build up your confidence.

Breaking Bad Habits That Keep You Scared

"It is easier to prevent bad habits than to break them."

— Benjamin Franklyn

Your habits play an important role in your success. We already know this, but the challenge comes in knowing which habits are good and which damage our lifestyle. Habits aren't good or bad unless they hold you back from achieving what you truly desire in your life.

If you want better health, obviously eating excessive amounts of junk food or smoking would be categorized as bad habits. Charles Duhigg, bestselling author of *The Power of Habit*, said: *The Golden Rule of Habit Change: You can't extinguish a bad habit, you can only change it.*

If we can't discern the good from the bad, we end up taking actions without thinking about what we are working for. When you climb the wrong ladder, it doesn't matter if you reach the top or not. This same principal applies to building better habits to put us on a more focused path.

In my years of experience, I have seen people continue to perform poorly, not from lack of skill or knowledge, but because they had poor habits that set them up for failure.

The problem is that we don't know what we don't know, and when it comes to habit formation, we don't know which habits are helping us and which are hurting us. Even sometimes when it feels like we are doing the right thing, that habit can be hurting our chances of getting ahead.

Our passive habits make us afraid to take action. These habits are automatic, and we feed them repeatedly throughout the day without any conscious effort. Passive habits may include:

- Sleeping in late because that is what you have always done.
- Spending money you don't have when you're bored.
- Watching TV for hours to avoid working.
- Scrolling through social media feeds looking for something interesting to entertain you.
- Eating junk food without any thought to how we will feel the next day.

Implementing Good Habits

For years, my habits kept me scared. We all have habits that we want to change, but without knowing what changes we want, creating better habits becomes more difficult. When you successfully change a habit, you aren't only making a shift in your actions, but also in your emotions. Adjusting the related habits can lead to a major shift in your emotions.

But, what exactly is a good habit? How do we define a bad one? Obviously, smoking is a bad habit due to the health risks, but to the person who smokes, the habit itself provides a sense of relief. They have formed an emotional trigger with the habit that signifies pleasure, relief, and the temporary removal of stress.

Here is an example of a good habit I have implemented: I write 2,000 words every morning for my blog and books. Because I implemented this habit, I have been able to produce over 40 blog posts this year and written seven books in the past eighteen months. With the development and consistent action of this one habit, I am now enjoying success as an author.

But it wasn't always this way.

For years, I spent my time watching TV and playing video games. I did everything except write, even though I had the desire to do it. But watching TV excessively or passing time with any other passive habit doesn't bring our dreams to life; it steals them away.

Bad habits were robbing me of what I really wanted. The only way to write my first book was to taper down my TV-watching time by 80 percent. I finally did this and got the work done. As a result, I felt more confident and that gave me the momentum I needed to work harder. This momentum led me to develop better habits in the morning and a stronger work ethic that changed my identity.

Just as practicing good habits can boost confidence, practicing destructive habits rob you of it. Here is an example:

Darie [a friend of mine] wants to lose weight. This has been her long-term goal for the past several years. She usually starts strong for the first month but loses interest and goes back to gorging.

When she was sticking to the diet, she lost several pounds but then returned to the damaging habit of eating crap again. Why? She felt great when she could see her progress, but, as everyone knows, it gets harder when you don't see expected results soon enough. Then we return to old ways of thinking and fall into comfortable routines so we will feel good about ourselves again.

Comfortable routines are predictable. We know what to expect from them. They rarely disappoint us because it is impossible to fail at them. But developing a new routine focused on a goal is a risk. We get scared of what could be and feel a strong pull to return to the predictability of a failed outcome.

What bad habits can you replace with good ones? What is it you hope to achieve with this new arrangement?

The Habits that Keep You Scared

For years, I had several habits that kept me scared and trapped. Procrastination was at the top of the list. I was always in the habit of neglecting what needed to be done. For example, creating a life plan, a financial plan, or mapping out my goals were all things I wanted to accomplish, but whenever I thought about them there was something more pressing to do.

Procrastination, while it felt like I was in control because I could make the decision to do or not do something, was robbing me of the life I could have had. The habit of doing it later became destructive. And, because I wasn't getting the things done that should have been, I was always scared of the future. Will I be okay? What if I run out of money? What is going to happen to my life?

When you develop the right habits, fear has no place in your life. To feel positive and enthusiastic about the future, we need structure and an organized plan, even if it is only a temporary one. Whenever I tried to act on my bad habits they would lead back to more procrastination. Then I'd experience a deep sense of fear that had returned. Bad habits are those that hold you back from achieving the impossible. You'll never be great with mediocre habits.

Right now, identify three bad habits you'd like to kick. Once identified, ask yourself: *why is it important for me to replace these habits with something else?* Without a strong enough answer, chances are you'll struggle to succeed at replacing them and eventually slip back into old routines, do what you've always done, and get what you've always gotten.

Five Steps for Breaking Bad Habits

Step 1: Recognize the Routine

Every habit has a place of origin. It thrives in a certain environment triggered by a stimulus. The routine is your way of feeding the habit. We give it what it desires the most: a reward. By feeding bad habits they are able to stay strong and control you.

A routine is a set of actions repeated consistently, often subconsciously. It is triggered by an external or internal stimulus in which we feel the need to feed this habit by giving into the impulse.

For most people, it is an addiction of some sort, such as smoking, checking email often, or compulsively shopping. Once you decide the course of action, it follows a set pattern and, if there is an emotional reward, you will continue to repeat the behavior.

Once you recognize the routine of your habit, you can implement a new set of actions to change it.

Step 2: Identify the Trigger

This is the point where we can catch our bad habit as it is stimulated by a trigger. This can be anything from an environmental trigger, watching something on TV, a feeling we suddenly get, or a certain person we meet.

The trigger, in this case, is the key. Once you identify what triggers you to take action, this is the point you are going to make a decision to either act...or not.

Your trigger is often an impulsive act. We don't think but react when it is switched on. It's purely compulsive. Addictions are formed through triggers. When we can recognize the trigger approaching, such as a craving for doing something, it becomes easier to turn it around.

Step 3: Replace the Action and Create New Behavior

If you make the conscious choice to not act when the trigger is activated, you have to replace the intended action [how you would normally react] with a new action. This new pattern, if repeated and implementing the replacement action, will form the new habit over a matter of weeks or months.

Just using willpower alone to try and not act out isn't enough. If you bare-knuckle it, you'll never recover. This is like an addict trying to kick the habit cold turkey without making attempts to replace the addiction. We need to know what the routine is, and then, when we are triggered to respond, be ready to take a different set of actions that break the habit.

For example: You might be triggered to buy something online because you are bored. How can you replace this? Step away from the computer as soon as the trigger hits you. Get busy with another activity. You could even shut down your computer for the night and do something else that will break the impulse.

Step 4: Focus on Small, Incremental Changes

Reframing a habit takes time. You won't reinvent all your habits right away, but you will if you repeatedly switch your triggers and make yourself aware of the areas in which you are weak.

If your habit is wasting time on social media when you could be doing more constructive things, create a plan and a system to move away from this habit. With so many distractions, wasting time on worthless activities is common.

The changes may be small, but any shift in your attitude, emotions, or actions is going to have a long-term impact if practiced consistently. This is how habits are formed, and this is how they can be reinvented.

Step 5: Focus on Your New Reward

There has to be a driving force behind change. Otherwise, what is the point? Earlier we talked about the Ostrich Approach and how we bury our heads in the sand to escape reality. This escape tactic is, in many ways, a reward for people.

We can avoid the current reality that is frightening, and live as if everything is just fine. But when we get real about what is actually happening in our lives and make changes, the rewards are revealed much later.

In the immediate gratification approach, you might feel good now because you're seemingly getting away with: paying your bills, having a discussion, or accepting an illness. But, the immediate gratification approach has poor long-term rewards. In the end, you end up losing more than if you had taken action in the beginning.

To change a habit, you have to see the reward that is to come, but it might take months or years before you see any results. That's okay. If it were easy, everyone would be doing it.

Think of it this way: even though you might be scared to set up a financial plan for yourself, ten years from now, your family will be so much better off if you start today. Always have the reward serve as a reminder of what is yet to come. Don't let it go. Keep it there in the front of your mind at all times.

Key Takeaways

Create a <u>Nothing Scares Me</u> Journal: *A System for Recording Your Victories.*

You can monitor your habit changing progress. Do this whenever a trigger moment occurs — when you are bored or meet someone that makes you want to react a certain way.

By not giving into this feeling, you have just gained points. Every time you say NO, it paves the way for a larger YES down the road.

When you create a journal, dedicate a section or page to one habit you are working on reinventing. Record your progress, changes made, and most of all, how you really feel about committing to this habit changing challenge.

Failing at What You Love to Do Best

"I can accept failure, everyone fails at something. But I can't accept not trying."

— Michael Jordan

There is a myth that people who successfully live a life of passion and do what they love, were born with some innate skill. We are disillusioned in thinking that the reason we are not yet successful is, merely, because we don't have what it takes, or that we were not born with the same talents.

You might catch yourself saying things like, *wow, she's lucky* or, *that guy has got to be some kind of creative genius.*

I have met many creative people in my life. They do have talent, skill, and a drive I admire. But they weren't necessarily born with it. It is a skill that has been practiced with love and persistence.

When you love what you do you will do anything to become good at it. Born a genius or not, every master has to practice what they love to do, even when they don't want to.

We hear success stories of online entrepreneurs who've created the next Facebook or revolutionary product, or of unknown authors suddenly striking it big with bestsellers they wrote overnight. No matter the field, I don't believe anybody is brilliant or lucky enough that they can just show up, perform, and get paid millions. It does happen on occasion, but for the majority of those who succeed at doing what they love, it is a combination of passion, perseverance, and organized planning.

What we may perceive as luck or talent is, hidden behind the curtain, a lot of hard work and drive. You *drive* forward in what you love, and push hard to master it.

What are you driving for right now? What pushes you through to do what you love? If you know the answer to this, you're a huge step ahead. When you do what you love and you work at it every day, you are building a platform for success. This may take one year, or it may take twenty.

We have to take action and do what scares us most so we can live our lives as thriving examples of our own unique genius. We can do this by doing what we love, and by doing it poorly at first.

When you successfully fail at what you love most, but continue to work and fail no matter how many attempts you make, then you've tapped into the secret formula.

The people who succeed at doing what they love will do what they have to do in order to master their passion, even when they don't feel like doing it. Taking action when you feel motivated isn't good enough. Motivation isn't always consistent. There is a deeper element in play that I call the *fear of regret*.

The Fear of Failing

We all have at least one regret. The things we wish we had done. The things we wish we'd said. But regret is grounded in the past. It ties you to a series of failed outcomes. This kills your confidence and drags down your self-esteem.

Self-esteem is something we need a lot of. If you are constantly focused on what could have been, it is impossible to focus on what could be. We should never trade in old memories for the chance to create new ones. In other words, we can create our future without repeating the same mistakes of the past.

Our motivation comes from focusing on what could be. It comes from the possibility of living your thriving lifestyle tomorrow, and not from the life you could have had. Abandon those thoughts that tie you to something that *can never be*. Get into the headspace of *what will be*.

Have you heard about Michael Jordan's practice sessions and the discipline he put into becoming the best basketball player on the planet?

Michael Jordan was cut from the high school basketball tryouts and told he'd never make it as a player. But he had grit, discipline, and a love for the game. Michael Jordan would show up hours before the game and practice hundreds of shots. Michael failed over and over. But his missed shots were necessary to push him to practice and carry his career to the top, helping him win the Most Valuable Player Award five times and lead the Bulls to six NBA championships.

> *"I've missed more than 9,000 shots in my career. I've lost almost 300 games. Twenty-six times, I've been trusted to take the game winning shot and missed. I've failed over and over and over again in my life. And that is why I succeed."*
>
> **— Michael Jordan**

Another example is 'master of horror' author **Stephen King**, who has written over 60 international bestselling novels to earn the *Bram Stoker Award* and *The Medal for Distinguished*

Contribution to American Letters. He has sold over 350 million books worldwide, but when he started writing he just wanted enough cash to pay for his rent. Fortunately, King loves writing. His habit of writing every day, even on holidays, eventually paid off to earn him a spot as one of the literary greats.

Why is it that we don't mind failing at work we don't like, but when it comes to work we love, we fear failing the most? If we refuse to fail at what we love, what else is there? And if we don't master what we love, what else is there?

When you learn to master the craft that is your true passion, you tap into the most diverse strength in your personal arsenal. When we commit to the process of winning first and stay that course, we can overcome any barrier that gets in the way.

I am always amazed that most people are willing to get up early, go to work for ten hours [including commute time], and then come home too exhausted to do the work that really matters. Yes, the reality is we have family, work and responsibility that has to be taken care of.

But what do you do when you are with real time on your hands? How do you spend those minutes or hours when you are free? Do you work on your passion, making time for it because it matters, or, would you rather watch television?

In many cases, it isn't that we lack time or motivation: it is commitment. Like Jordan, we have to get up early and commit to making the shots, hit or miss. It is the action of doing it that makes the difference.

If you have a passion you're hiding from the world, what are you waiting for? Permission to start building your dream? Nobody is going to give you permission to start living your dream. You are the one who has to jump in and take it. If you are waiting for the perfect time, you'll regret it years later, saying, "If only I had…"

Michael Jordan wasn't afraid of failing; he was only afraid of not doing what he loved. This is the case with many people. We are in a position where we work for other people and try to do a good job so we qualify for that paycheck. Then, when we get that paycheck, we feel validated, rewarded, fulfilled.

But it never lasts.

One of the surest roads to happiness is by doing what you love, and the only way to get there is by taking action, overcoming adversity, and charging ahead without looking back.

People are desperate to do what they love, but the problem is this: they are either too busy, or they don't yet know what it is they want to do so they do whatever job comes along. You might pay your bills by doing work that doesn't matter, but you'll always be poor if you end up with regret.

My big scare came one day when I realized nobody but me was in charge of my life. You see, for many years, I leaned on others for support. If I was in a relationship, I looked to that person for happiness. They never lasted because the relationship couldn't sustain my needs. What did I do then? I looked for another relationship. It was an endless series of failures. So, what is the definition of failing? Doing the same thing over and over again and expecting to get a different result. It never was different.

In past jobs I worked for a paycheck like everyone else. But, at the end of the month, having rewarded myself for a job well done by drinking away most of my earnings, I had more days left than cash. This is how we learn to fail, and keep on failing.

You know that Edison guy who loved to play with electricity? The story is, he failed 10,000 times. But by the end he had a successful product. Edison obviously had a massive amount of motivation to be persistent. If you can fail that many times and not give up, you are onto something. But we don't need to fail thousands of times. Just a few, or ten or twenty may be enough.

Show me a success story not riddled with failure. It doesn't exist. But I know many failures who never tried, and ended up burned-out, living futile existences for somebody else. If you enjoy working for someone else, building their brand, selling their products, and making money for them, then stop reading this book. Go back to doing that.

Or, if you are ready to stand up and take action towards doing the things you love, let's get to it.

Now...

Think about the amount of work the average person [you and I] put into working for other people or organizations. If you are doing work you don't like, you'll never get better at it unless you're forced to do so. Maybe your boss threatens to replace you if you don't meet sales goals. Or, maybe you won't get that promotion unless you can sign the contract with a big client.

I don't know much, but I do know this: work you love needs no prompting. You don't have to be threatened or be given ultimatums to succeed at what drives you. Was Jordan forced to play basketball? No, he chose to play, and he decided to put in more effort than others.

When Stephen King was asked, "Why did you become a writer?" he responded with, "You think I had a choice?"

When we are made to do something, we don't put half as much effort in as we do when we're born to do it.

So now…

- Figure out what you love to do more than anything else. Invest your time on mastering this.
- Work out solutions to the obstacles that are holding you back.

The Four Rules for Succeeding at What You Love

(1). Commit to mastering your craft.

Spend time everyday working on the skill, technique, and know-how of your real work. Mastery doesn't mean perfection. It is what can be achieved with a lifetime of practice. We have to practice or there isn't any progress.

We master our passions by choosing to do whatever it takes to become better. If you have no time for practice, when can you find the time? I've heard people tell me all the plans they have for their lives after they retire. After they retire? What if you don't make it that far?

Many people die before they reach sixty. And if you do retire at that age, how motivated will you be to suddenly start working on your real dream? The time is now. The best time was yesterday, but if you're still thinking about finding the perfect time to get started, let me put this to rest right now.

Start today. Forget about *someday*. Life is full of someday promises. Someday I'll start that business; someday I'll take that trip; someday I'll change, and yes, someday we're all going to die. You might die with all those *someday* promises banked up.

(2). Benchmark your success against someone else.

Then, go above and beyond what they are doing. Pick someone you know that is succeeding at what you want to do. Make a list of their achievements and read about their successes and strategies so you can emulate what they've done.

Entrepreneur and the nation's #1 leading business strategist Tony Robbins said that we could achieve mastery by emulating those that have achieved what we want. This doesn't mean you'll get the same results—you probably won't—but doing what others do isn't a bad thing. Following in the footsteps of a successful person is much better than leading and being followed by twenty fools. You can benchmark your success by setting milestones for your work.

(3). Stay consistent with your practice.

Before we are good at something we have to be really bad at it. But many people start things they fail to stick with. I did this throughout my life and it became a bad habit I struggled to change.

Creating a consistent habit that focuses on learning one new skill is the key to mastery. Consistent practice with small improvements beats the 'I have to do this perfectly or else' way of thinking.

If you want to be a blogger, you have to post regularly and be satisfied with getting it done, even when it's not perfect. If you practice the guitar, you can focus on learning just one new chord a week. Practice just that one chord for thirty minutes a day. If cooking is your passion, make the same recipe every day for thirty days, tweaking it slightly differently each day so that you make gradual improvements to the taste.

Consistency, doing something regularly in small increments, is better than doing it once for four hours every other week.

We only master the things we pay attention to.

(4). Identify the areas that need the most attention and improvement.

One of the mistakes we make is recognizing what we can do well and doing more of it, while overlooking our weaknesses and convincing ourselves to let it go.

The master of any craft needs to be aware of what they do well and what needs improvement so they can excel at what they want to do. It isn't always fun or glamorous, but we have to work on our weaknesses as well as our strengths. This is how you carve out a life that is great instead of just good enough.

You don't want to settle for good enough. When we take the low road, and convince ourselves we have learned enough, we stop learning altogether. When we continue to learn, because we know that the world is unlimited, we keep making progress. When we move forward, we find fulfillment, satisfaction, and more happiness. Who doesn't want to be happy?

Key Takeaways

- Focus in on your true passion. Schedule thirty minutes a day to practice your craft.
- Fail at your passion and fail consistently. Our mistakes are stepping stones to progress.
- Don't settle for good enough. Identify the weaker areas of your life and focus on making it better.
- Develop the attitude of *I'm doing it now* instead of *I'm living scared*.

Practicing Limitless Thinking

"Keep on going and the chances are you will stumble on something, perhaps when you are least expecting it. I have never heard of anyone stumbling on something sitting down."

— Charles Kettering

Your thoughts are your most powerful tools. Everything you have and don't have can be linked back to your quality of thinking. Your limitations are directly linked to your thoughts. Just as you can limit yourself, the opposite can also be true. You can develop an abundance mindset, and when you believe anything is possible, your thoughts and the lifestyle they create become limitless.

But remember: just as positive thoughts can raise you up and make you feel like you're on top of the world, negative thoughts can drag you down to the bottom of the barrel. Negativity is the main source of fear. Positivity is the removal of fear.

Go Limitless

When you are in a negative state of mind, everything becomes twice as hard because you feed into your limitations and give them power. This is why we need to move away from negative thoughts and the people, places, and things that create them.

But don't just take my word for it; let's try an exercise. Clear your mind of whatever you are thinking right now. Sit in silence for five minutes. Now, think of something that excites you. Whatever it is, get passionate about it. Let it fire you up. Hold nothing back. Visualize yourself doing things that you once thought were impossible. When you can visualize yourself doing it, you will do it. Your vision for living a limitless lifestyle spills over into the real world.

For example, I am thinking about taking a family vacation. I can do this because I have my own business – all I need is my laptop and imagination. No cubicle, and no boss. When I think about this, I feel excited because I know it is possible. Several years ago, this was one of those impossible dreams. I was tied to a job with little vacation time. I couldn't afford to go. There wasn't time for that.

The limits that are forged in my mind become reality. Every time. This is an important lesson. If anything prevents you from taking action now, it is the limiting beliefs that say, *this isn't for you*, why don't you go do something more realistic.

But realism is dangerous. When we judge our dreams against the bar of what is reality, we push ourselves into a funnel of limitations. For example, to say that I will earn three thousand dollars next month is possible. It isn't a challenge because anybody can do this. But to say I'll be earning twenty grand a month one year from now is, from the start, an unbelievable goal when it is grounded in reality. Why? Reality exists because someone else set the bar and they expect us to live by it.

When nothing scares you, go ahead and raise the bar accordingly. You decide what it is that's possible. You set your limitless boundaries. You challenge the reality that has been decided by the world and all its systems.

To be limitless, we must challenge the 'normal' way of thinking and set our beliefs outside the comfort zone. Most people won't do this. They're afraid to fail. But wouldn't you rather fail at something that is challenging and builds a new future than fail at what you hate doing? You can be limitless in your decisions and beliefs.

What is your biggest goal in life?

Is there someone you love and want to spend more time with?

Would you like to take a trip?

Is there a job you've hesitated to apply for but want more than anything? Can you visualize yourself in this position doing the work you love?

Now, write down an idea, dream, or concept that you've always believed is *beyond your current reality.* This should be a goal or life dream that appears to be beyond your reach. For example, maybe you want to create a company that earns you one million dollars a year, write a bestselling book, or travel the world as a digital nomad.

If you want to test your limitless thinking, tell people about your next big goal. You can quickly weed out the naysayers who will tell you it isn't possible. People will tell you it can't be done until somebody does it. When someone says this, just remember, what they mean is that it's not possible for them. But, for you, it is doable.

Becoming a limitless thinker doesn't require any special talent or ability. Remember: we are trained to think within our own limitations. When I was in school, many years ago, teachers told me what I could and couldn't do. Over time, if you believe in your limitations, every decision you make will be followed by a weak action. You'll never push yourself any further than you believe you are capable of.

Distance Yourself from Naysayers

People who are unsupportive of your limitless lifestyle and holding you back have no place in your life. You have two choices. You can: 1. Join them or 2. Distance yourself from them.

Hanging out with negative people makes you negative. When you are exposed to streams of negativity on a regular basis, even if it isn't by choice, you absorb the bad energy it sends your way. Naysayers stick together. If you are in a situation where you have to associate with them, distance yourself from them as much as possible.

People who grew up in negative, limiting environments struggle most of their lives to create a limitless mindset. It becomes a major hurdle to overcome an environment that focuses on promoting mediocrity and living within set boundaries and limitations. But this doesn't mean your life is an impossible gambit. You have the power to change your thoughts and emotions. You can't always change your environment, but you can control your reaction to it.

The same can be said for your work atmosphere. Each office has an overall culture that is created by the company executives, employees, and

SCOTT ALLAN

environment this may harm or help you. Again, we
can't always choose the people we work with, but
we can choose our attitude towards the situation.
Your attitude is the one thing you have complete
control over, regardless of other people who may
drag you down.

Practice Limitless Mainstreaming Every Morning

Your thoughts are most influential first thing in
the morning. In fact, if you wake up with thinking
negative thoughts they might stick with you for
the rest of the day. Start the day off right, and
you'll have a much better chance of maintaining a
positive mood throughout the day.

Spend the first 20 minutes of your day developing
your thoughts and plans for the day. Here is what
I do: block off twenty minutes after you first wake
up. This is, possibly, the most important twenty
minutes of your day. The quality of your day
hinges on *how you wake up*.

Instead of rolling out of bed late and grabbing
your smartphone, we are implementing a new
strategy. This will change everything and build the
foundation for limitless thinking.

In Hal Elrod's bestselling book, *The Miracle
Morning,* he introduces the Life S.A.V.E.R.S.

practices. I use the S.A.V.E.R.S. methods of **S**ilence, **A**ffirmations, **V**isualization, **E**xercise, and **R**eading to improve my thoughts for the day. Check out *The Miracle Morning* and put these strategies into practice.

I set up my limitless thinking for each day by **setting my thoughts straight before bed.** The last thought you had before crawling under the sheets is the first thought you'll have when you wake up. So, if you want to wake up early and make the most of your time, work on your thoughts for ten minutes before bed.

Four Simple Strategies

Go into Silence. Play a deep and relaxing piece of music. My favorite is *Weightless* by Marconi Union. Then, let your thoughts drift. This is a form of meditation but, instead of trying to think of nothing, you think of the good things in your life. This is how you can go into silence while making everything around you perfectly calm. The day's arguments, problems, and challenges can be washed away.

Start with Gratitude. Who do you feel deep gratitude for being in your life? What do you feel grateful for? Run through the most important people in your life. Think about them and send them positive thoughts.

I suggest you start each day with a gratitude list. It can be one thing or ten. Focus on the good people and things that are worth working for. Without gratitude, it's hard to practice a limitless way of life.

Self-Talk with Positive Affirmation. Over the years I have practiced recounting quotes and affirmations to change my thinking. This has a powerful impact on the way your mind functions. As I mentioned already, we all come with our own *self-talk radios* pre-installed in our minds.

Over the years, this radio gets louder and the noise increases with experience. If we don't closely monitor it, our radios can [and will] turn our thoughts into negative messages that impact our mental health.

An affirmation is a phrase that can change your beliefs. They work because we get so stuck in our own thoughts that we forget to correct course. The messages that we listen to become repetitive over time until we believe them. You have the power to choose your thoughts. Positive affirmations can help.

Read a Good Book. Kick-start your day by reading and thinking positively in the morning. If you start your day right, you'll do most things right. Start it badly, by focusing on resentment, and you'll feel like shit. Worse yet, you'll build fear and resentment into everything you do. Fear causes us to act out irrationally without thinking of the consequences.

Limited vs. Limitless

To expand your freedom and choices, you need to expand the limitless possibilities you believe in. It isn't so much what you believe, but how strongly you believe in it. Likewise, it isn't what you think, but how positively you think it. Abundance thinking, or limitless thinking, focuses on growth. Limited thoughts keep you scrambling for more because you feel restricted and limited to what is possible.

Our self-created limitations set the bar for success in all segments of our lives: financial matters, relationships, work, and personal development. By staying limited you are deciding how big, how far, and how much you can transform your life.

A limited thinking person struggles to come up with an occupation that pays six figures; whereas limitless people find new ways to increase income streams and work to reach their goal of a six-figure salary.

Building Abundance

Limited people live in a world of scarcity. They believe life is about holding onto their possessions. When they learn something, they'll keep it to themselves so nobody can take their idea and profit from it.

If you live in scarcity, there is never enough money, time, or material things to keep you satisfied for long. Scarcity is about hoarding and skimping. Limitlessness is about giving and sharing. If there is any single mindset that creates a constantly fearful state, it is the mindset of scarcity.

Limitless people are focused on abundance. They believe the world is full of treasures, and that there is more than enough for everyone. There is enough money, food, shelter, and love to go around.

Abundant people live happier, healthier lives. They have little fear. When they do, the right people usually surround them. If you focus on the abundance and richness of what you have, and you grasp the large opportunity that is available, you'll see it is easy to create an abundant way of thinking. Abundance is, after all, a way of life, and has little to do with owning anything.

Key Takeaways

- When we are limitless in our thoughts, we also become limitless in our actions.
- Your actions will always follow your thoughts, so make your thoughts a positive driving force to get you to do things that matter most to you.
- Abundance isn't about having stuff, but, rather, giving stuff away. It isn't about owning, but about letting go. And it's not always about being the best, but about striving to make the best of a situation.
- Let go of scarcity thinking. It has no place in your life. Embrace the limitless lifestyle that is yours to create.

Rejecting the Life You Don't Want

> *"The greatest day in your life and mine is when we take total responsibility for our attitudes. That's the day we truly grow up."*
>
> **— John C. Maxwell**

In our day-to-day lives, it feels like everything is just happening around us without our input or effort. But actually, we create most of what is happening, even if it is at a subconscious level. Believe it or not, you have the power to structure everything to happen for you instead of to you.

In other words, we can be intentional about building the life we want. This is far better than accepting the life we've just fallen into by default.

For years, I lived passively and by default — I would just *go with the flow* or *take whatever comes*. The problem with this approach is that you give up control of the main events that shape, mold and transform your life. When I realized I was my life's creator and not just a passive participant reacting to circumstances, everything changed.

I learned to reject the life I no longer wanted. This included getting up every day, getting dressed, and commuting one hour to an office so I could sit at a desk and play with a computer. This meant no longer doing *their* work that I hated. Believe me, when you make the conscious choice to do something about your life's direction, it changes it all.

When you reject the life you have for the life you truly want, your mindset shifts from a passive state to pro active. In other words, you seize control of your life. This is something many people fail to do. We struggle, give up, fight some more, try to push through, and when we feel the pressure to conform, many of us feel defeated.

If this has happened to you, it's not your fault. Life can be tough. We try to keep our heads above water, but sometimes we're pushed below the surface. Instead of thriving we end up drowning in worry, stress, and the possibility of failure.

The Life You Build When You're Scared

We live in one of two realities: living scared or doing it scared. If you are still living scared, chances are somebody or something else has locked you into a life that has been crafted for their purpose. Again, it's not all your fault, so before you blame yourself for creating a bad situation, let's focus on turning it around.

I've been there many times. There are days when I am still caught in the tumultuous river of life and I think everything is pushing me under and that I'll never succeed. When I am trapped by my fear, I build a life and make choices that keep me stuck.

But, if I tap into the abundance that I am creating, I build the opposite lifestyle. When you take responsibility for where you are at, it becomes a journey with greater clarity. Instead of guessing what you should be working for, you know what it is you need to do.

Living scared creates hesitation. You feel uncertain about what you should be doing. You're afraid to take that next step for fear of screwing up, looking bad, or acting stupid. Feeling trapped, we stick to the safer path, but there is danger in safety for the fearful.

To live with less fear and gain greater courage for doing it scared, we must begin with intention.

This brings us to…

Building an Intentional Lifestyle

Many years ago, I found myself living a life that was no longer aligned with my dreams or future goals. My dream was still taking shape, but what I did know was that the life I had wasn't the life I wanted. So what did I do? I rejected the life I had made and set out to create a new one.

Oprah Winfrey did this. Born into poverty in Mississippi, she knew she didn't want to be trapped living the life she'd been born into, wearing potato sacks in place of clothes. Instead of accepting it, Oprah did something about it. She set out to carve her own destiny by becoming the world's most successful and wealthiest TV talent. None of this was by accident. Her life was built by intention. She knew precisely what she wanted and, more importantly, she knew what she didn't want.

Knowing what we don't want is as powerful as knowing what we do want. For example, maybe you want to write for a living and be a bestselling author, but you are currently working a job you don't like. The work isn't what you want to do. You know you want out, and by deciding, with intention, that you are going to break free and do the work you love, you create momentum to make changes and move toward doing the work you love.

Your intentional actions lead to desired results. When people do what is expected of them, because somebody else demands it, they lose that intentional mindset. But, staying focused on what you really want, even when others are trying to direct you, is how you break out of the life you don't want.

When you find yourself stuck in a situation that you had no intention of creating, then it's time to…

Saying NO to What You Don't Want

This is the key to rejecting the unwanted stuff that is thrown at you. Like prisoners forced to eat whatever is given to them, we think we have no choice in what life is offering. Do not settle for what you can get but rather, set out to attract and obtain those things that you really desire.

If you are not saying *yes* to what you want, you are saying *no* to what you do want. By saying *no* more often, you can stop saying *yes*. For years, I would say *yes* just to get along with people: my employer, my spouse, and even people I didn't know.

I would try to please people to earn their approval and look for their acceptance to feel complete. But this robs us of our personal freedom. Creating a lifestyle that is intentional has to start with intentional choices. It is easy to believe that we have no choices when, in reality, we have lots of choices.

But we limit ourselves to believing that *I have to do this* or *if I don't do this, someone will get upset.* You need to be crystal clear about what your actions lead to. This is intention. You have a desired outcome that you'll never reach if you play it safe all the time. When we play it safe to please somebody else, we risk more of our happiness in the long run.

A friend and mentor once said to me, "When you rock the boat, someone always gets wet. So, what are you waiting for? Tip that thing over!" What he meant was, if you want to get real results, you will have to break some eggs, but that's okay. It's better than walking on eggshells.

Take responsibility for your life: Yes, *your* life. Begin by recognizing the power of your decisions. You can choose, decide, and initiate action. If someone or something is getting in your way and keeping you from creating an intentional lifestyle, this is an obstacle that must be removed. When we fail to try to move the barriers in our life, we stay stuck in our ruts.

But, when you do things differently, not everyone likes the changes you make. Some people liked the old you; they needed you to hang out at the bar with them and complain about the misery of life. But when you shift your actions, it creates change.

Courage is born from change, and change can come from courage.

Don't just settle for what you can get. Decide what you want, decide what you are willing to give up to get it, and then create a **massive action** game plan for getting it.

What to Do When You Are in Doubt

If you doubt what you are doing, ask someone you trust who has the success you are striving for. Don't ask the person who is failing their way through life. Ask the person you want to emulate — a mentor or coach — who is doing what you want to be doing. Ask someone who is leading with intention. Get real answers from the people who are leading by example. You can only succeed if you model success.

Streamlined actions in alignment with your intentional outcome won't fail you. But, follow the path of confusion and doubt and you'll encounter fear everywhere you turn. Fear is the result of not knowing if what you are doing is right or wrong. When you are not in control, meaning that something else is deciding your fate, you can expect to be fearful of today, tomorrow, and all the days to follow.

You have the power to reject the life that has been handed to you. We are not victims of our circumstances, but the masters of it. You control your future by managing your thoughts and actions. Manage them well because if you don't, somebody else will.

Key Takeaways

- Rejecting the life you don't want is about saying *no* more than you say *yes*. You have to say *no* to the people, situations, and distractions that steal your time and freedom.
- Confusion and chaos become your masters when you can't control your environment.
- Be intentional in your choices, actions, and behaviors.
- Choosing intentional direction puts you in charge of your life. What you do with intention directs your purpose.
- Focus on the obstacles blocking your path and discuss with your mentor the solutions for handling difficult situations.

What Would My Life Be Like If…?

"Dream small dreams. If you make them too big, you get overwhelmed and you don't do anything. If you make small goals and accomplish them, it gives you the confidence to go on to higher goals."

— John H. Johnson

In a workshop I attended several years ago, the facilitator asked us a question: "What would you do with your life from this day forward if you were no longer afraid?"

The next question was more shocking: "Where would you be in your life today if you had taken action years ago instead of living scared?"

We all knew the answer. We'd be someplace else doing what we love instead of in a workshop trying to figure it out. But it didn't matter. We were all on a journey together and, we all had to start where we were at that moment. At that time, I was with a group of other people trying to figure out where we would like to be in the not-too-distant future.

To break it down even more, we had to come up with specific scenarios that were holding us back. Some people feared starting a business, racing a triathlon, speaking in public, or meeting new people. The people who joined the seminar were all suffering from some form of *hold back*. They wanted to change or do something significantly different with their lives, and yet, something held them back from taking action.

Here is an example. One of the attendees, Bob, wanted to travel around the world, but he had never traveled before. He was afraid of planes and didn't even have a passport. He said that he always found lots of excuses to stay scared and do nothing. Over the course of the next day in the workshop, as each of us analyzed the fears that were keeping us scared to act, here is what we found out:

All of us agreed that we were focused on the big picture scenario. For example, several people wanted to start their own businesses but when they thought about all the work ahead—hiring employees, technical issues—they felt overwhelmed and would procrastinate. This was a common thread. We would visualize the outcome but lose sight of the small steps that lead up to it.

So how do you climb the world's tallest mountain?

You start from the base.

One step at a time.

One foot in front of the other.

You get there by keeping it simple.

Creating an If-Then Plan

To accomplish anything, you have to break down the action steps into bite-sized manageable chunks. This is the first stage to realizing your big goals.

In Bob's case, he wanted to travel, but he would have panic attacks when he thought about visiting other countries. So, he broke the process into manageable chunks. These were small steps he could focus on.

Instead of worrying about what he would say when he got to security at the airport, he would focus on the next step, such as applying for a passport or checking out the travel packages that he could purchase for his trip.

So, here's a list of his initial steps:

Step #1: Go to the passport office. Get a passport.

Step#2: Take a short trip on an airplane to a neighboring state.

Step #3: Research the first country to visit – only the first one.

Step#4: Make a list of activities and sites to see in that first country.

During this process, we were instructed to ask ourselves: "What if I just…" So in Bob's case, "What if I just get my passport first? What then?"

Getting a passport isn't a big deal; it's a relatively simple process. You don't have to think about the 30 countries you want to visit. That comes later. Just focus on the one thing that is getting you closer to that goal.

In many cases, people ask the wrong questions. They ask themselves scary questions that keep them from doing anything. For example, I used to ask myself: "What will happen if I fail? What will happen if I take the test and don't make it? What will happen if I lose money?" Every negative question receives a fearful answer.

But you can turn this around to your advantage as well.

What would happen if I lost money? Well, I would learn a valuable lesson. And besides, money can be replaced.

What would happen if I failed? Well, I'd learn what not to do next time. Or, maybe I'd discover a new way to fail. Every failure, as we've learned, is success in disguise. We learn by failing, and we can succeed faster by knowing what doesn't work.

If you imagine your actions failing, you'll never do anything. This is why people stay stuck. They are too frightened to move forward. Would you take action if you were convinced you'd lose money or something worse? Maybe not. But turn that vision into something positive and you can find a way.

What would happen if I…

- Made that phone call?
- Filled out that application form?
- Met that new person who is interested in a date?
- Tested out that new idea?
- Tried to implement that new habit?
- Signed up for the course?
- Visited the bank to enquire about house loans?

Don't hold back because you are scared. Everyone is scared. We're all afraid to fail, afraid to look stupid, or afraid to imagine the possibilities. But, people take incredible chances every day. They go beyond their comfort zones and do things that seriously impact their lives.

So, the question is: *what are you going to do today?*

What is on your *what would happen if I...* list?

Nobody has all the answers for what they should be doing with their life. But, you can think deeply about what your next step should be by asking yourself the question: *what would life be like if...* Then you can start to visualize the life you want to create.

We can't undo the past, but we can create a better tomorrow. We can create a future and all the things that come with it just by deciding. Once you decide, *commit* to your objectives. Know what your dream is. Then, *execute* your plan with massive action.

Finding Your Dominoes Trigger Point

Several years ago I was introduced to what is called the *domino effect*: one action can trigger everything else to fall into place.

Or, in the case of dominoes, one action [the first domino to fall] impacts all the other steps that follow [the rest of the dominoes fall]. When you take one action, it leads into another.

Soon you are full of **confidence** and you feel **unstoppable**. But it starts with taking action towards that first task.

Now, identify the *one thing* you can do to set off the series of actionable steps.

Here are some examples:

You want to write a book but you've been putting it off. So, you create a simple mind map. This leads to an outline. The outline leads to the first paragraph, page, and eventually the completion of the first chapter.

You want to run in a marathon, but you're a terrible runner. So, you set a goal to run five minutes, or 200 meters on the first day. The next day, you run 500 meters. You keep building on your previous day's goal until you are up to 5 km.

You want to start your own blog, but all the steps involved overwhelm you. So, first you register for a domain name. Then, you sign up for hosting. Then you watch a video on how to write your first blog post.

You want to travel, to expand your mind, and explore places you've only dreamed of, but you're afraid to get on that airplane. Can you imagine what would happen if you did?

I love the idea of reinventing and transforming one's life into what it could be instead of settling for what it is. When we stay scared and love scared, we settle for what is. There is no growth.

No stimulation. We need to take action and make a difference.

Change is always frightening. But what is scarier is not changing, staying stagnant, and failing to pursue your life goals because you're afraid of what might happen.

If you were being chased by a lion right up to the edge of a cliff, and your only chance of survival was to jump, you probably would. In times of stress we take action to survive. But daily life isn't much different. We should jump into unknown waters so we can find out what is on the other side of our fear.

Again, all of this is possible if you keep asking yourself: *what if I just…* And then you go and do it. This could be considered your most difficult task for the day as well. If you are going to start your day right, why not start by taking action towards your dream.

You have nothing to lose and nothing to fear.

What would you do if you finished this book and discovered the secret to setting your dreams on fire?

Let's find out.

Key Takeaways

- Make a list of actions you have been meaning to take and ask yourself: *how would life be different if I did this thing?*
- What are you scared of trying? What negative outcome are you holding onto? Turn this outcome into something positive and see how it affects your emotions.
- What is the one massive step you could take that would trigger your dominoes effect?
- Make a list of things that you can do by asking yourself: *What if I just…*
- Think baby steps. Take small, incremental actions towards your goal. Focus on moving forward just a little bit one small step at a time.

Tackling Your Most Difficult Tasks First

"Permanence, perseverance and persistence in spite of all obstacles, discouragements, and impossibilities: It is this, that in all things distinguishes the strong soul from the weak."

— Thomas Carlyle

An important part of the *Nothing Scares Me* formula is tackling the tasks, projects, or actions you have identified as most difficult and doing them first. When we take care of the tough stuff before anything else, we can exponentially reduce our level of fear. This eliminates procrastination and builds real momentum for the road ahead.

Working Through the Tough Stuff First

It is always easier to do the little things first — to do what is easy and then make time for the more difficult projects later. There is logic in this plan, but it fails for several reasons. First of all, we are creatures of comfort. The only time we do the tough stuff first is when we are forced to.

- Your boss gives you a deadline and makes you do that report by Friday.
- The bank tells you to pay your bill by this date or else they will cut off your credit.
- You have until this Friday to make that all-important call or you lose the deal of a lifetime.

In examining the things that you've swept under the rug, you may find a lot of projects, tasks, and forgotten deadlines. These tasks were left behind because, for one reason or another, we didn't want to do them.

I know what it is like when you have to do a job or task you don't want to. Let's be honest, when we don't want to face the reality of a situation, we will find a way to get around it. Most people take the *Ostrich Method* that I mentioned at the beginning of this book, when they are faced with difficult tasks. It is always *easier* to turn away when faced with a difficult challenge. We want to pretend it isn't there, as if by avoiding it, somehow it will just *take care of itself*.

People who deny their fear become a slave to it. Even if you ignore reality, it will still hit you full force one day, knocking you down for good. This is why getting into the habit of doing tough tasks first will make you mentally sharper, reduce anxiety, and increase your confidence in ways that you've never experienced. But it starts with you pulling your head out of the sand.

For years, I lived like an ostrich. I avoided tasks I didn't want to do. This included everything from controlling my finances to applying for a new passport. There were times I had to organize my life so I could function more efficiently, but I continued to put it off. The result: confusion, stress, fear, and personal anarchy.

You will never find peace by trying to escape your reality. There will always be something pulling at you when you leave business unfinished. Unfinished business can be anything from clearing your house of clutter to setting up your online business. If something sticks in your mind and refuses to leave, it's an indication that it needs to be done. If you're a procrastinator who fears taking action, this chapter is for you. Keep reading.

How Can I Finally Take on Difficult Tasks I've Been Avoiding?

Each night you could make a list of the top five tasks you want to get done the next day. Then, choose the toughest thing on your list. This is easy to determine because it's the one you don't want to do but must get done. You will try to resist this one thing the most. You'll find excuses not to do it and try to do the easy tasks first. Then the tough task will get moved down the ladder until, eventually, it's put aside until it rears its ugly head again.

Taking care of tough business reduces the fear factor exponentially. I suffer from severe stress and worry when I put things off that need to be done. You can lose sleep, lose hair, and lose money, too. But it doesn't have to be this way. The after effect of doing what scares you is powerful. The act of completing something gives you new perspective. You prove to yourself that the fear of starting was what you were hiding from.

My Simple System for Getting Difficult Tasks Done

First of all, it comes down to how you identify your action steps. If this were something that could be done in thirty minutes, I would do it right away. But some of our tough tasks require in-depth planning, systematic organization, and weekly goals. This is why we put things off: we have too many things to think about in a world full of distraction.

Worse yet, the things I was neglecting were important, but I continued to chase the *easy rabbits*, thinking I was making progress. What feels like efficiency is, at times, really the illusion of covering up what should be done in favor of what we want to do. When you develop the habit of *Doing It Scared*, you put yourself on a course to achieve your goals faster, and focus your energy on more important projects while eliminating the unnecessary. You can stop wasting valuable time on the activities that matter least.

Start with Your Project List

As David Allen writes in his book, *Getting Things Done,* a project is anything that requires more than three steps. If we have a set of tasks we need to perform, set aside time every day, even if it is just ten minutes, to knock off the mini-goals to get the big project done.

But first, you need to *make a list of projects*. What is on your plate that will be completed with a series of steps? Chances are there is a list of multiple action steps to go along with each project. Without knowing what needs to be done, we can easily get bogged down and overwhelmed. Then, the cycle of doing things by default is picked up again.

Here is a list of projects that are hovering over my head and filling my mental space with clutter.

Create a new website. I procrastinated for almost one year, potentially costing myself thousands of dollars by having no place to sell products or services.

Write a book. I have always wanted to write a book. Although I have five written now, this was a huge undertaking when I started mostly because I feared the rejection that could come from selling a real product.

Declutter my home. There is nothing worse than wading through junk every day. And it's easy to turn a blind eye and just toss stuff in the corner. Clutter creates stress, and stress leads to fear, worry, and anxiety. This is a major project, but the more you tackle it, the easier it becomes.

There are many tasks we put off because they are difficult, but the main reason we stress is scarcity.

I was always afraid of starting things I could not follow through, or of becoming overwhelmed by the amount of work and giving up.

To get cracking on the difficult tasks holding you back, create a list. It is this list that is going to show you what you have been neglecting. Now, this is not a to-do list. We don't want to make a list of things we should be doing [such as picking up the groceries or signing up for Netflix]. This is the list of what scares you. There should be nothing easy on it. The golden rule is that when you struggle or don't want to put something on this list you need to.

A to-do list is simple. We usually write down tasks we'd like to do, and they are usually unproductive. Your *tough tasks* list is different. It should make you uncomfortable. Mine did. But as I approached each obstacle, and set out to tackle the action steps for each project, I became empowered in a way I want you to feel.

So, Let's Get to It…

You can use software to record and track your steps, or plain old pen and paper. I may be old fashioned, but I like pen and paper. There is something about writing it down that makes it more real. Write your list and tack it up on your wall. Don't file it away where you can't see it or you'll forget about it within a week.

Start your list with a mind dump of all the difficult tasks you have been putting off, neglecting, or avoiding. This list needs to be a hard version of the truth.

Maybe you've been putting off having a serious conversation with someone because you don't want to rock the boat or cause trouble. Once again, if it's on your mind, it needs to be done. No exceptions. This work is, perhaps, the most important task-based activity in this book. I don't say that lightly. When we take action in the *moments we feel scared,* it builds greater courage to confront uncomfortable situations.

When I decided to do the stuff I'd avoided for years, it was as if I was setting myself free. The things that you bury, even though they may benefit you in the long run, are not going to disappear. Remember, life is going to pass even if you choose the ostrich approach and bury your head in the sand. You can hide but you can't escape.

So, make your list. Then divide it into two parts. After you complete your brain dump, take a look and see what tasks are actually projects. Then, create a folder for projects. If you are writing this down, use a whole sheet of paper for each project. Like I said, I get more out of it if I write everything in a notebook. You can type it up later if you want.

Now, a project is anything that requires multiple steps. If you want to set up a website for an online business, this requires several steps and weeks of work. Maybe you've been avoiding it because tech stuff scares you, or you are worried that after you get it all done nobody will come knocking on your virtual door. I know, the fear holds you back, but I encourage you to push forward. You'll only regret it if you don't try.

You can make another list for actions that can be completed in less than thirty minutes. If you have several projects, you'll have a lot of action tasks that will take thirty minutes or less. But, we want to do this separately. Individual items that can be completed [and that are not projects] can be on your other list.

Now You Have Two Lists — One for Short Tasks, One for Projects

The project lists will work like this. You are taking a 30,000-foot view of the scope of this project, and you'll spend some time mind dumping actions required to complete the project. Depending on the scope of the project this may take some time, but this is the best way to get this done. Then, you can easily show up every day, pull out your list of action tasks, and put your plan into action.

For years, I avoided doing certain projects because I was clueless about what actions needed to be taken. I was looking at the project as a huge behemoth that existed in my mind only. Without an organized plan, you'll struggle to tame your scared factor. There is nothing like getting things done and feeling that sense of deep accomplishment that comes with completion.

So, if you are ready, get to work creating your action plan. This doesn't have to be finished today, but this is what I recommend.

If you follow my advice, you'll nail this.

Set aside one day – one *whole* day. Dedicate it to mapping out your projects, writing action plans, and determining how many hours will be required to get it done.

Doing it in one day is better than stretching it out over several days or weeks. I discovered that, when I didn't do it in one day, it dragged on for months, and, eventually, I stopped altogether and nothing got accomplished.

Block off one day to make a master list of both:

1. Projects + action items for each project;

2. Tasks that can be finished in 30 minutes or less.

That is it.

By making this exercise a priority, you'll reduce your fear, feel less scared about waking up in the morning, and gain greater control over a part of your life that has been out of control.

Key Takeaways

- Create a master list of your difficult projects and tasks.

- Set aside an entire day for this work.
- Choose the project you are going to work on first.
- Make sure it is one that you've been putting off.

Building Confidence
(The "Brick-by-Brick" Builder Strategy)

> *"Action is a great restorer and builder of confidence.
> Inaction is not only the result, but the cause, of fear.
> Perhaps the action you take will be successful; perhaps
> different action or adjustments will have to follow. But
> any action is better than no action at all."*
>
> **— Norman Vincent Peale**

In this final chapter of *Nothing Scares Me,* I'll share with you the **four barriers** that defeat your confidence. Then, I'll follow up with the **six strategies** you can implement to increase your confidence to an all-new level.

But first, it is critical that I explain the key foundation of building and maintaining a life of confidence. There are four things we need to deeply consider when focusing on confidence building:

1. Confidence building is an internal job. Yes, your environment and the world around you have a heavy influence, but, at the end of the day, you are responsible.

2. Confidence building is a system of slow gains [more on this in a few pages].
3. Confidence is a learned condition. We can train ourselves to be as confident as we want. How confident would you have to be to tackle your biggest goal this year?
4. Confidence must be grounded in reality. If you tell yourself you are a super athlete and that you're in great shape in order to boost your confidence, but, in fact, you smoke and are overweight, you have to bring yourself down to reality and start with the truth of where you are.

> *"Confidence is, after all, your ability to believe in yourself. It is the highest form of self-esteem. Without believing in what it is you want to achieve, you'll fail to achieve it. When you believe, it kicks your internal power into hyper drive. A powerful belief can overcome any obstacle and pave the way for better things to come your way."*
>
> **— Patrick King**

I'm going to share with you some powerful but simple strategies for building confidence. But first, 5 obstacles that get in the way of confidence development.

The Four Obstacles That Kill Confidence

I've suffered from a lack of confidence most of my life. I used to think I was born with some kind of ailment that nobody else had, because I had very little confidence in anything. I would read stories about brave people and how they overcame insurmountable obstacles to achieve their dreams.

Later, after a lot of self-searching, I discovered that it wasn't the lack of anything that was the problem, and my external environment had very little to do with it. It's what I was holding onto that was killing my confidence.

The barriers I created in my own mind were holding me back. It was then I realized that change always happens on the inside first.

Although we are influenced by external events that we have little control over, we have total power over the internal conditions that govern our thoughts and feelings.

When we struggle to overcome a barrier in our lives, in most cases, the walls are built on the inside. This is where we keep our fears and doubts locked away. When you can recognize the obstacles in your way as something you created, it is easier to remove them.

Here are four obstacles that could be holding you back from being more confident.

1. Uncertainty & Self-doubt

Having little faith in our capabilities or skills, we fill ourselves up with feelings of doubt and uncertainty. We use language like, *I can't do this* or, *how will I ever get through this?* When you have an image of yourself as someone who *can't*, this means you usually won't. As I already discussed in chapter 7, self-doubt can be turned into confident action by doing what you are afraid of.

The courage is on the other side of your actions. When you are feeling uncertain and doubtful of what you should do next, it's an indication that fear is holding you back. In all likelihood, if you question your self-doubt, you may discover that it is being created by your lack of belief.

2. Perfectionistic Thinking [all-or-nothing]

This kills your confidence because it prevents you from ever starting anything. Perfectionism is closely tied with procrastination. When we fear not doing it perfectly, we begin to fantasize about what it would be like if we did do it. Or worse yet, you are waiting for the perfect moment before taking action.

But as we now know, the only path to building real confidence that sticks is to do it: 1. When you are scared, and 2. Frequently. Confidence isn't something you can build up by dreaming about it,

NOTHING SCARES ME • 177

and you'll never have that perfect condition or situation. The time is and always has been right NOW.

3. Focusing Only on the Big Win

Can you imagine if the only time you ever felt good about yourself was when you accomplished something BIG. For example, you might feel confident after making that huge sale, but what about all the little sales you had to make to build up to it? We often dismiss the little steps we take to get to where we want to be.

Before you can run a full marathon [42.195 km], you have to be able to run five km, then ten, and eventually build yourself up to running the entire distance. But those little distances are, in fact, goal achievements. Getting closer to the BIG goal builds your confidence along the way. The road to success, whatever that may be, is littered with small victories.

4. Believing In F.E.A.R.

When we believe that our fears are greater than we are, it makes them larger than life. Our fears are not bigger than we are but, believing that they can defeat us, adds weight to the illusion of fear. Throughout this book I discussed several anecdotes to overcoming our fears and doubts and, to keep fear in perspective, we need to look at this way.

Fear is nothing more than **F**alse **E**vidence **A**ppearing **R**eal. Many of the future events we are convinced will happen rarely do. Sure, bad stuff does happen, and in many cases the things we never feared could happen too.

For example:

- You lose a job you were convinced was secure. What are you going to do?
- Your spouse walks out on you after twenty years of marriage. What are you going to do?
- The market crashes overnight and you lose 90% of your investments. What are you going to do?

The truth is, we waste too much time dreaming up fears of the future that may or may not happen. But who can predict what is going to happen today, tomorrow or in twenty years from now? There is no evidence to prove that 99% of our fears exist. The imagination is great at conjuring up illusions of what could happen.

The fear of failure? Yes, you will fail.

The fear of loss? Yes, you will lose something at least once in the next decade.

The fear of dying? Yes, that will happen too. Not today but, you can take great comfort in knowing most of your fears are false and some are destined to happen no matter what.

Our fears are only as great as our imaginations allow them to be. By knowing you can take action and make choices in the present moment, it fills your mind and spirit with confidence.

Building Confidence

This is, what I like to call, the **brick-by-brick method of confidence building**. For every mini-action you take, no matter how minuscule it may be, you are adding a small brick to your house of confidence. A home is really the combination of thousands of parts all glued, nailed, and pasted together. Those parts all got put together because somebody took the time to ensure every piece was installed.

What we can do, when it comes to building confidence, is, take a small action each day. This builds confidence while reducing the fear factor. And fear thrives in an environment when the person feels helpless, paralyzed, hopeless or out of control.

In **Barrie Davenport's** book *Building Confidence* she says:

> *"Your self-esteem is based on your beliefs about your own inherent values as a person and your emotional view of those beliefs. You can certainly lack confidence and still have self-esteem. It's much more difficult to lack self-esteem and still feel confident about yourself and your abilities."*

Now, here are six strategies you can use to build your confidence, take action, and do the things you've always wanted to.

Strategy #1: Model the Confidence of Confident People.

Confidence is not just a one time and it's over event. It is an ongoing process and self-development. No matter how confident you are, there is always someone who is more so. They have more confidence because they are operating on a different level than you. They may be more experienced, wiser, more positive, or more influential in their fields. This is a good thing. It means that we can get there, not by achieving one massive win, but by achieving a series of small and incremental wins over a period of time.

By modeling the people who are achieving the incredible success we would like, we set the bar and push ourselves to reach for it. For example, I have fear of public speaking. When I get up on the stage in front of a crowd, fear grips my chest and I can barely breathe. BUT, I can build confidence in public speaking by watching others do it. How do they perform? What voice control are they using? How are they thinking in that moment as they are up on stage?

I can learn to be confident on stage by emulating the speeches of others – like by watching YouTube videos and then practicing in the mirror. You can apply this strategy to anything you desire to master and gain greater confidence.

You want to write a book but have no confidence in your writing? Read a book by your favorite author and then write a page on your thoughts about that book. Modeling isn't about copying but watching how others do it and then trying it ourselves with a twist of our own to make it unique.

Strategy #2: Start Small, Aim High.

Stephen Guise has written a book called *Mini-Habits*. In the book he discusses how we can get more done and achieve our goals, by doing things that matter and taking action in small bite-sized chunks.

By breaking down the process into smaller, manageable pieces, we reduce that overwhelming feeling of trying to achieve a major goal or break a bad habit. This also helps with building

SCOTT ALLAN

confidence of course because we can feel better about ourselves when we achieve each little goal.

Strategy #3: Practice to Fail First

In most cases we are so afraid to fail that we avoid trying. Our expectations and attitude from the get-go is: I have to be perfect before I try this. When we think this way, it reduces our motivation and drive to try. We defeat ourselves by refusing to practice and learning to fail.

If you play something, like the piano or guitar, you know that it takes years of failing and practice before you feel confident enough to play in front of a crowded room. Nobody gets it right the first time.

If you don't give yourself that room to grow, you'll never develop the skills you need to become confident. Learning to fail is essential. You need to give yourself permission to learn. Confident people are not born, they are made through years of trial and error.

Strategy #4: Perform the Small Stuff with Consistency

The next strategy is a combination of the first two but is a necessary element in the confidence formula. As I mentioned, confidence building is a consistent series of actions performed gradually over time. We build confidence by doing, regardless of the outcome. You will try many things and fail, but that also makes you stronger.

By performing small steps regularly, as in conditioning for a full marathon, your confidence is kicked up a notch with each mini-win. Don't stay focused on the big picture [finishing a full marathon], but on the bite-sized goals you have to hit to get there –such as running your first 2km.

The other key to this is that the action has to be consistent. If you are only practicing when you feel like it or are motivated to, confidence levels will fall. And if you fail to achieve your BIG WIN, such as completing that marathon, it will register as a failure in your mind. Stay consistent in your actions and set up a regular schedule for taking action.

Strategy #5: Focus on Confident Relationships

The people you hang out with, as we discussed in Chapter 3, have powerful influence on your confidence. If you are hanging with doubters and negativity mongers, you can expect to function at their level of self-esteem.

Make time for people who fill you up with that loving feeling and are good influencers. These people are your key relationships. You can gradually cut the people who keep you stuck loose.

These are the complainers, the people with heavy baggage, and the energy drainers. Cut them loose. Focus on the people who support and encourage your success. Recognize who they are and schedule quality time with them.

Strategy #6: Make a List of Your Good Stuff

Confidence is built when we focus on the positive aspects of our lives. You should start every week with a list of the five things you consider to be most important. Is it your family? Your health? Your business? What do you feel deep gratitude for? What makes you feel good?

You can start energizing your confidence right away by making a list of the people and things that you are grateful for. Gratitude is powerful. It puts the positive into perspective.

Go ahead and make your list right now. Then, let it be the first thing you read every morning. As time goes on, add to this list. Make it a goal to come up with a list of 100 items.

The Cost of Having Low Confidence

You have to ask yourself: *what is having a lack of confidence actually costing me?* Think about this for a minute. When we lack the confidence we need to reach out to people, we are missing out on valuable relationships that could help us on the journey. I'm a firm believer that nothing matters more than the relationships you develop along the way.

Developing confidence takes time, but it doesn't have to become a major project. It isn't something that you do just once and then forget about for the rest of your days.

Confidence building involves staying on track with your values, taking consistent small actions, and persevering to make gradual progress in relationships, work, and fun. Self-confidence is an inside job. You get there by working from the inside out.

This book is packed with enough to fill up your confidence meter and keep you charging forward and enjoying life.

Remember to laugh.

Enjoy what you have.

Reach out to others.

Give away what you have.

You can achieve anything by teaching other people how to reach their dreams, too.

186 • SCOTT ALLAN

Key Takeaways

- Most obstacles we encounter are created from the inside. You have complete control over the internal barriers holding you back.

- Most external situations are created by events beyond our control, and focusing on the barriers you can't destroy is a waste of time and effort.

- Self-doubt can be turned into confident action by doing what you are afraid of.

- The best time to act is NOW. In taking action we condition ourselves to push through even when we are faced with heavy resistance. If you're not moving forward, you are being held back.

- You can increase confidence by modeling confident people. How do they speak, act and perform?

- Build your confidence in learning to fail. Success is not the only way to become more confident. We get this way through attempting what we are afraid of, regardless the outcome.

- Stick with your values and take small, consistent actions every day until you get to where you want to be.

CONCLUSION

Weighing the Risks of Staying Scared

*"Most people talk about fear of the unknown, but if
there is anything to fear, it is the known."*

– Deepak Chopra

We have come to the end of the book, but your
journey is just beginning. Confronting your fears
takes courage. Taking action, even when you are
met with heavy resistance, is a matter of pushing
forward with courage.

The people who persevere, stick to their plans,
and take small steps to reach their goals, are the
winners who never quit. As you will see, anyone or
anything that tries to hold you back will fail. The
quality of your lifestyle is everything. There is
nothing you can't do when you stay committed to
a course of action.

What are You Giving Up to Stay Scared?

188 • SCOTT ALLAN

As I promised, now that you have finished this book, you are ready to do anything. Nothing is standing in your way except *you*.

Anything worth having requires an element of discomfort. It means facing the things that scare us, and it requires working through your fears on a consistent basis. Never stop learning. Welcome the discomfort of being scared and doing something about it.

I want you to know that there is no shame in being scared. We all have fear. What matters is what we do with that fear. Will you stand back and let it control you? Or, will you get out there and take charge of your life by doing what needs to be done?

You know by now that you are capable of achieving anything. But don't take my word for it. Take action and get results. Don't be afraid to **live larger than life**.

What Action Should I Take?

First, make a list of all the things you've been putting off. Areas of procrastination point to something you fear — you either fear starting it, doing it, or completing it.

As part of your *Nothing Scares Me* action plan and to hold yourself accountable each day, I encourage you to do what you are afraid to do. Take a real look at your life, and, observing yourself carefully, take note of the tasks and situations you are avoiding. How would your life be different if you take action today, and do something that you have always been afraid to do?

By using this method, I have seen people leave jobs they hated, divorce abusive and controlling partners, and make total life changes by changing their bad habits, unhealthy behavior and self-defeating daily rituals. In order to change your life, you have to shift your approach to life.

Decision drives behavior. Behavior forges character. Character is mastered when we push through our greatest struggles.

Focus on Your Gains and Not the Goal

Every little success is a victory. But when we are working toward our dreams, it is easy to focus on the end goal. The problem is that it makes the journey seem too long. This journey is never-ending. I hope you'll never stop growing, pushing forward, and working towards your life-long ambition, whatever that may be.

As you grow, change, and develop, remember to focus on the small gains. Measure your success with the little stuff you accomplish every day. I find that when I focus on the big picture, I become overwhelmed with multiple action tasks that appear endless.

Keep track of the small stuff you get done. When you do something that challenges a fear or pushes you closer to your goal, that mini-victory is big. No matter what you are striving for, you can only get there by taking a series of small leaps and bounds.

I don't know a lot but I do know this: our lives are short, and some are much shorter than others. This is why we must appreciate every day. You were brought into this world for a reason. Aren't you the least bit curious to know what it is?

I know I am, and I try to uncover a bit of this treasure every day. I try to discover something new and do what part of me may want to resist creating more abundance in my life and the lives of others.

Don't stop jumping. You can sit on the ledge and look off in the distance toward what you have yet to climb, but, sooner or later, you have to start moving. Don't stop pushing forward. Break your resistance and seek help in the areas of your life that you struggle with.

Be afraid but courageous.

You've got this.

One step at a time…

Scott Allan

BEFORE YOU LEAVE…SUBSCRIBE TO MY FREE WEEKLY NEWSLETTER AND JOIN THE COMMUNITY OF 30,000+ LIFETIME LEARNERS!

Click here to subscribe or scan the QR code below.

"When you walk to the edge of all the light you have and take that first step into the darkness of the unknown, you must believe that one of two things will happen. There will be something solid for you to stand upon or you will be taught to fly."

– Patrick Overton

Books Change Lives.
Let's Change Yours Today.

Check out the complete
Bulletproof Mindset Mastery series here by Scott Allan.
Visit author.to/ScottAllanBooks or scan the QR Code
below to follow Scott Allan and stay up to date on future
book releases

Begin Your Rejection Free Journey Today!
RejectionFreeBooks.com

Pathways to Mastery Series

Master Your Life One Book at a Time

Available where books and audiobooks are sold

About Scott Allan

Scott Allan is an international bestselling author of 15+ books in the area of personal growth and self-development. He is the author of **Fail Big**, **Undefeated,** and **Do the Hard Things First**.

As a former corporate business trainer in Japan, and Transformational Mindset Strategist, Scott has invested over 10,000 hours of practice and research into the areas of self-mastery and leadership training.

With an unrelenting passion for teaching, building critical life skills, and inspiring people around the world to take charge of their lives, Scott Allan is committed to a path of constant and never-ending self-improvement.

Many of the success strategies and self-empowerment material that is reinventing lives around the world evolves from Scott Allan's 20 years of practice and teaching critical skills to corporate executives, individuals, and business owners.

You can connect with Scott at:

ScottAllan@scottallaninternational.com

Visit author.to/ScottAllanBooks **to stay up to date on future book releases.**

Printed in Great Britain
by Amazon

10695549R00119